The Essential Bu

Jaguar/Daimler
XJ 1994-2003
All models (inc VDP)

Your marque expert:
Peter Crespin

VELOCE PUBLISHING
THE PUBLISHER OF FINE AUTOMOTIVE BOOKS

Other great books from Veloce –

Speedpro Series
4-cylinder Engine – How To Blueprint & Build A Short Block For High Performance (Hammill)
Alfa Romeo DOHC High-performance Manual (Kartalamakis)
Alfa Romeo V6 Engine High-performance Manual (Kartalamakis)
BMC 998cc A-series Engine – How To Power Tune (Hammill)
1275cc A-series High-performance Manual (Hammill)
Camshafts – How To Choose & Time Them For Maximum Power (Hammill)
Competition Car Datalogging Manual, The (Templeman)
Cylinder Heads – How To Build, Modify & Power Tune Updated & Revised Edition (Burgess & Gollan)
Distributor-type Ignition Systems – How To Build & Power Tune New 3rd Edition (Hammill)
Fast Road Car – How To Plan And Build Revised & Updated Colour New Edition (Stapleton)
Ford SOHC 'Pinto' & Sierra Cosworth DOHC Engines – How To Power Tune Updated & Enlarged Edition (Hammill)
Ford V8 – How To Power Tune Small Block Engines (Hammill)
Harley-Davidson Evolution Engines – How To Build & Power Tune (Hammill)
Holley Carburetors – How To Build & Power Tune Revised & Updated Edition (Hammill)
Jaguar XK Engines – How To Power Tune Revised & Updated Colour Edition (Hammill)
MG Midget & Austin-Healey Sprite – How To Power Tune New 3rd Edition (Stapleton)
MGB 4-cylinder Engine – How To Power Tune (Burgess)
MGB V8 Power – How To Give Your, Third Colour Edition (Williams)
MGB, MGC & MGB V8 – How To Improve New 2nd Edition (Williams)
Mini Engines – How To Power Tune On A Small Budget Colour Edition (Hammill)
Motorcycle-engined Racing Car – How To Build (Pashley)
Motorsport – Getting Started in (Collins)
Nitrous Oxide High-performance Manual, The (Langfield)
Rover V8 Engines – How To Power Tune (Hammill)
Sportscar & Kitcar Suspension & Brakes – How To Build & Modify Revised 3rd Edition (Hammill)
SU Carburettor High-performance Manual (Hammill)
Successful Low-Cost Rally Car, How to Build a (Young)
Suzuki 4x4 – How To Modify For Serious Off-road Action (Richardson)
Tiger Avon Sportscar – How To Build Your Own Updated & Revised 2nd Edition (Dudley)
TR2, 3 & TR4 – How To Improve (Williams)
TR5, 250 & TR6 – How To Improve (Williams)
TR7 & TR8 – How To Improve (Williams)
V8 Engine – How To Build A Short Block For High Performance (Hammill)
Volkswagen Beetle Suspension, Brakes & Chassis – How To Modify For High Performance (Hale)
Volkswagen Bus Suspension, Brakes & Chassis – How To Modify For High Performance (Hale)
Weber DCOE, & Dellorto DHLA Carburetors – How To Build & Power Tune 3rd Edition (Hammill)

Those Were The Days ... Series
Alpine Trials & Rallies 1910-1973 (Pfundner)
Austerity Motoring (Bobbitt)
Brighton National Speed Trials (Gardiner)
British Lorries Of The 1950s (Bobbitt)
British Touring Car Championship, The (Collins)
British Police Cars (Walker)
British Woodies (Peck)
Dune Buggy Phenomenon (Hale)
Dune Buggy Phenomenon Volume 2 (Hale)
Hot Rod & Stock Car Racing in Britain In The 1980s (Neil)
Last Real Austins, The, 1946-1959 (Peck)
MG's Abingdon Factory (Moylan)
Motor Racing At Brands Hatch In The Seventies (Parker)
Motor Racing At Brands Hatch In The Eighties (Parker)
Motor Racing At Crystal Palace (Collins)
Motor Racing At Goodwood In The Sixties (Gardiner)
Motor Racing At Nassau In The 1950s & 1960s (O'Neil)
Motor Racing At Oulton Park In The 1960s (McFadyen)
Motor Racing At Oulton Park In The 1970s (McFadyen)
Three Wheelers (Bobbitt)

Enthusiast's Restoration Manual Series
Citroën 2CV, How To Restore (Porter)
Classic Car Bodywork, How To Restore (Thaddeus)
Classic Car Electrics (Thaddeus)
Classic Cars, How To Paint (Thaddeus)
Reliant Regal, How To Restore (Payne)
Triumph TR2/3/3A, How To Restore (Williams)
Triumph TR4/4A, How To Restore (Williams)
Triumph TR5/250 & 6, How To Restore (Williams)
Triumph TR7/8, How To Restore (Williams)
Volkswagen Beetle, How To Restore (Tyler)
VW Bay Window Bus (Paxton)
Yamaha FS1-E, How To Restore (Watts)

Essential Buyer's Guide Series
Alfa GT (Booker)
Alfa Romeo Spider Giulia (Booker & Talbott)
BMW GS (Henshaw)
BSA Bantam (Henshaw)
BSA Twins (Henshaw)
Citroën 2CV (Paxton)
Citroën ID & DS (Heilig)
Fiat 500 & 600 (Bobbitt)
Jaguar E-type 3.8 & 4.2-litre (Crespin)
Jaguar E-type V12 5.3-litre (Crespin)
Jaguar XJ 1995-2003 (Crespin)
Jaguar/Daimler XJ6, XJ12 & Sovereign (Crespin)
Jaguar/Daimler XJ40 (Crespin)
Jaguar XJ-S (Crespin)
MGB & MGB GT (Williams)
Mercedes-Benz 280SL-560DSL Roadsters (Bass)
Mercedes-Benz 'Pagoda' 230SL, 250SL & 280SL Roadsters & Coupés (Bass)
Mini (Paxton)
Morris Minor & 1000 (Newell)
Porsche 928 (Hemmings)
Rolls-Royce Silver Shadow & Bentley T-Series (Bobbitt)
Subaru Impreza (Hobbs)
Triumph Bonneville (Henshaw)
Triumph TR6 (Williams)
VW Beetle (Cservenka & Copping)
VW Bus (Cservenka & Copping)
VW Golf GTI (Cservenka & Copping)

Auto-Graphics Series
Fiat-based Abarths (Sparrow)
Jaguar MKI & II Saloons (Sparrow)
Lambretta Li Series Scooters (Sparrow)

Rally Giants Series
Audi Quattro (Robson)
Austin Healey 100-6 & 3000 (Robson)
Fiat 131 Abarth (Robson)
Ford Escort MkI (Robson)
Ford Escort RS Cosworth & World Rally Car (Robson)
Ford Escort RS1800 (Robson)
Lancia Stratos (Robson)
Mini Cooper/Mini Cooper S (Robson)
Peugeot 205 T16 (Robson)
Subaru Impreza (Robson)

General
1½-litre GP Racing 1961-1965 (Whitelock)
AC Two-litre Saloons & Buckland Sportscars (Archibald)
Alfa Romeo Giulia Coupé GT & GTA (Tipler)
Alfa Romeo Montreal – The Essential Companion (Taylor)
Alfa Tipo 33 (McDonough & Collins)
Alpine & Renault – The Development Of The Revolutionary Turbo F1 Car 1968 to 1979 (Smith)
Anatomy Of The Works Minis (Moylan)
Armstrong-Siddeley (Smith)
Autodrome (Collins & Ireland)
Automotive A-Z, Lane's Dictionary Of Automotive Terms (Lane)
Automotive Mascots (Kay & Springate)
Bahamas Speed Weeks, The (O'Neil)
Bentley Continental, Corniche And Azure (Bennett)
Bentley MkVI, Rolls-Royce Silver Wraith, Dawn & Cloud/Bentley R & S-Series (Nutland)
BMC Competitions Department Secrets (Turner, Chambers Browning)
BMW 5-Series (Cranswick)
BMW Z-Cars (Taylor)
BMW Boxer Twins 1970-1995 Bible, The (Falloon)
Britains Farm Model Balers & Combines 1967 to 2007 (Pullen)
British 250cc Racing Motorcycles (Pereira)
British Cars, The Complete Catalogue Of, 1895-1975 (Culshaw & Horrobin)
BRM – A Mechanic's Tale (Salmon)
BRM V16 (Ludvigsen)
BSA Bantam Bible, The (Henshaw)
Bugatti Type 40 (Price)
Bugatti 46/50 Updated Edition (Price & Arbey)
Bugatti T44 & T49 (Price & Arbey)
Bugatti 57 2nd Edition (Price)
Caravans, The Illustrated History 1919-1959 (Jenkinson)
Caravans, The Illustrated History From 1960 (Jenkinson)
Carrera Panamericana, La (Tipler)
Chrysler 300 – America's Most Powerful Car 2nd Edition (Ackerson)
Chrysler PT Cruiser (Ackerson)
Citroën DS (Bobbitt)
Classic British Car Electrical Systems (Astley)
Cliff Allison – From The Fells To Ferrari (Gauld)
Cobra – The Real Thing! (Legate)
Cortina – Ford's Bestseller (Robson)
Coventry Climax Racing Engines (Hammill)
Daimler SP250 New Edition (Long)
Datsun Fairlady Roadster To 280ZX – The Z-Car Story (Long)
Diecast Toy Cars of the 1950s & 1960s (Ralston)
Dino – The V6 Ferrari (Long)
Dodge Challenger & Plymouth Barracuda (Grist)
Dodge Charger – Enduring Thunder (Ackerson)
Dodge Dynamite! (Grist)
Donington (Boddy)
Draw & Paint Cars – How To (Gardiner)
Drive On The Wild Side, A – 20 Extreme Driving Adventures From Around The World (Weaver)
Ducati 750 Bible, The (Falloon)
Ducati 860, 900 And Mille Bible, The (Falloon)
Dune Buggy, Building A – The Essential Manual (Shakespeare)
Dune Buggy Files (Hale)
Dune Buggy Handbook (Hale)
Edward Turner: The Man Behind The Motorcycles (Clew)
Fast Ladies – Female Racing Drivers 1888 to 1970 (Bouzanquet)
Fiat & Abarth 124 Spider & Coupé (Tipler)
Fiat & Abarth 500 & 600 2nd Edition (Bobbitt)
Fiats, Great Small (Ward)
Fine Art Of The Motorcycle Engine, The (Peirce)
Ford F100/F150 Pick-up 1948-1996 (Ackerson)
Ford F150 Pick-up 1997-2005 (Ackerson)
Ford GT – Then, And Now (Streather)
Ford GT40 (Legate)
Ford In Miniature (Olson)
Ford Model Y (Roberts)
Ford Thunderbird From 1954, The Book Of The (Long)
Forza Minardi! (Vigar)
Funky Mopeds (Skelton)
Gentleman Jack (Gauld)
GM In Miniature (Olson)
GT – The World's Best GT Cars 1953-73 (Dawson)
Hillclimbing & Sprinting – The Essential Manual (Short & Wilkinson)
Honda NSX (Long)
Jaguar, The Rise Of (Price)
Jaguar XJ-S (Long)
Jeep CJ (Ackerson)
Jeep Wrangler (Ackerson)
Karmann-Ghia Coupé & Convertible (Bobbitt)
Lamborghini Miura Bible, The (Sackey)
Lambretta Bible, The (Davies)
Lancia 037 (Collins)
Lancia Delta HF Integrale (Blaettel & Wagner)
Land Rover, The Half-ton Military (Cook)
Laverda Twins & Triples Bible 1968-1986 (Falloon)
Lea-Francis Story, The (Price)
Lexus Story, The (Long)
little book of smart, the (Jackson)
Lola – The Illustrated History (1957-1977) (Starkey)
Lola – All The Sports Racing & Single-seater Racing Cars 1978-1997 (Starkey)
Lola T70 – The Racing History & Individual Chassis Record 4th Edition (Starkey)
Lotus 49 (Oliver)
Marketingmobiles, The Wonderful Wacky World Of (Hale)
Mazda MX-5/Miata 1.6 Enthusiast's Workshop Manual (Grainger & Shoemark)
Mazda MX-5/Miata 1.8 Enthusiast's Workshop Manual (Grainger & Shoemark)
Mazda MX-5 Miata: The Book Of The World's Favourite Sportscar (Long)
Mazda MX-5 Miata Roadster (Long)
Maximum Mini (Booij)
MGA (Price Williams)
MGB & MGB GT– Expert Guide (Auto-doc Series) (Williams)
MGB Electrical Systems Updated & Revised Edition (Astley)
Micro Caravans (Jenkinson)
Micro Trucks (Mort)
Microcars At Large! (Quellin)
Mini Cooper – The Real Thing! (Tipler)
Mitsubishi Lancer Evo, The Road Car & WRC Story (Long)
Montlhéry, The Story Of The Paris Autodrome (Boddy)
Morgan Maverick (Lawrence)
Morris Minor, 60 Years On The Road (Newell)
Moto Guzzi Sport & Le Mans Bible, The (Falloon)
Motor Movies – The Posters! (Veysey)
Motor Racing – Reflections Of A Lost Era (Carter)
Motorcycle Apprentice (Cakebread)
Motorcycle Road & Racing Chassis Designs (Noakes)
Motorhomes, The Illustrated History (Jenkinson)
Motorsport In colour, 1950s (Wainwright)
Nissan 300ZX & 350Z – The Z-Car Story (Long)
Off-Road Giants! – Heroes of 1960s Motorcycle Sport (Westlake)
Pass The Theory And Practical Driving Tests (Gibson & Hoole)
Peking To Paris 2007 (Young)
Plastic Toy Cars Of The 1950s & 1960s (Ralston)
Pontiac Firebird (Cranswick)
Porsche Boxster (Long)
Porsche 356 (2nd Edition) (Long)
Porsche 908 (Födisch, Neßhöver, Roßbach, Schwarz & Roßbach)
Porsche 911 Carrera – The Last Of The Evolution (Corlett)
Porsche 911R, RS & RSR, 4th Edition (Starkey)
Porsche 911 – The Definitive History 1963-1971 (Long)
Porsche 911 – The Definitive History 1971-1977 (Long)
Porsche 911 – The Definitive History 1977-1987 (Long)
Porsche 911 – The Definitive History 1987-1997 (Long)
Porsche 911 – The Definitive History 1997-2004 (Long)
Porsche 911SC 'Super Carrera' – The Essential Companion (Streather)
Porsche 914 & 914-6: The Definitive History Of The Road & Competition Cars (Long)
Porsche 924 (Long)
Porsche 928 (Long)
Porsche 944 (Long)
Porsche 964, 993 & 996 Data Plate Code Breaker (Streather)
Porsche 993 'King Of Porsche' – The Essential Companion (Streather)
Porsche 996 'Supreme Porsche' – The Essential Companion (Streather)
Porsche Racing Cars – 1953 To 1975 (Long)
Porsche Racing Cars – 1976 To 2005 (Long)
Porsche – The Rally Story (Meredith)
Porsche: Three Generations Of Genius (Meredith)
RAC Rally Action! (Gardiner)
Rallye Sport Fords: The Inside Story (Moreton)
Redman, Jim – 6 Times World Motorcycle Champion: The Autobiography (Redman)
Rolls-Royce Silver Shadow/Bentley T Series Corniche & Camargue Revised & Enlarged Edition (Bobbitt)
Rolls-Royce Silver Spirit, Silver Spur & Bentley Mulsanne 2nd Edition (Bobbitt)
Russian Motor Vehicles (Kelly)
RX-7 – Mazda's Rotary Engine Sportscar (Updated & Revised New Edition) (Long)
Scooters & Microcars, The A-Z Of Popular (Dan)
Scooter Lifestyle (Grainger)
Singer Story: Cars, Commercial Vehicles, Bicycles & Motorcycle (Atkinson)
SM – Citroën's Maserati-engined Supercar (Long & Claverol)
Subaru Impreza: The Road Car And WRC Story (Long)
Supercar, How To Build your own (Thompson)
Taxi! The Story Of The 'London' Taxicab (Bobbitt)
Tinplate Toy Cars Of The 1950s & 1960s (Ralston)
Toyota Celica & Supra, The Book Of Toyota's Sports Coupés (Long)
Toyota MR2 Coupés & Spyders (Long)
Triumph Motorcycles & The Meriden Factory (Hancox)
Triumph Speed Twin & Thunderbird Bible (Woolridge)
Triumph Tiger Cub Bible (Estall)
Triumph Trophy Bible (Woolridge)
Triumph TR6 (Kimberley)
Unraced (Collins)
Velocette Motorcycles – MSS To Thruxton Updated & Revised (Burris)
Virgil Exner – Visioneer: The Official Biography Of Virgil M Exner Designer Extraordinaire (Grist)
Volkswagen Bus Book, The (Bobbitt)
Volkswagen Bus Or Van To Camper, How To Convert (Porter)
Volkswagens Of The World (Glen)
VW Beetle Cabriolet (Bobbitt)
VW Beetle – The Car Of The 20th Century (Copping)
VW Bus – 40 Years Of Splitties, Bays & Wedges (Copping)
VW Bus Book, The (Bobbitt)
VW Golf: Five Generations Of Fun (Copping & Cservenka)
VW – The Air-cooled Era (Copping)
VW T5 Camper Conversion Manual (Porter)
VW Campers (Copping)
Works Minis, The Last (Purves & Brenchley)
Works Rally Mechanic (Moylan)

www.veloce.co.uk

First published in February 2009 by Veloce Publishing Limited, 33 Trinity Street, Dorchester DT1 1TT, England. Fax 01305 268864/e-mail info@veloce.co.uk/web www.veloce.co.uk or www.velocebooks.com.
ISBN:978-1-84584-200-0/UPC: 636847042004
© Peter Crespin and Veloce Publishing 2009. All rights reserved. With the exception of quoting brief passages for the purpose of review, no part of this publication may be recorded, reproduced or transmitted by any means, including photocopying, without the written permission of Veloce Publishing Ltd. Throughout this book logos, model names and designations, etc, have been used for the purposes of identification, illustration and decoration. Such names are the property of the trademark holder as this is not an official publication.
Readers with ideas for automotive books, or books on other transport or related hobby subjects, are invited to write to the editorial director of Veloce Publishing at the above address.
British Library Cataloguing in Publication Data – A catalogue record for this book is available from the British Library. Typesetting, design and page make-up all by Veloce Publishing Ltd on Apple Mac.Printed in India by Replika Press.

Introduction & thanks
– the purpose of this book

Though based on the preceding model, the X300 was not merely a face-lifted XJ40*, the improvements were much more than skin deep. Though it lasted only 3 years until the V8 X308 models arrived, the X300s had, and continue to have, great appeal, and are arguably the last of the genuinely owner-serviceable Jaguar 6-cylinder cars. The V8s, when they came, were undoubtedly a better car in terms of refinement, power and even frugality, but reliability problems for the first few years blighted their reputation, and the interior styling was not to everyone's taste. The X300s also included the last of the Jaguar V12s (X305) and whilst these can be supremely reliable, they can prove an expensive money-pit if you buy the wrong car.

This book weighs up the pros and cons for all models and should help you decide which, if any, X300/308 model to buy.

The 94-97 6- & 12-cylinder cars, and the '97-2003 V8s, are complex vehicles. They do feature built-in diagnostic systems to help prospective purchasers highlight any faults, but they are still not a car to be purchased casually. This book works step-by-step through the various systems and structures, to give you an objective basis for evaluating any potential purchase. Jaguars always were, and remain, intoxicating cars, and to drive one is usually to fall in love with one. However, even at today's prices you need to spend with your head as well as your heart. That's where this book can help. These were expensive cars when new, and comparatively expensive to run. They may be much cheaper now but the running costs will be higher, as significant components come to the end of their useful life.

The X300/308 benefited from Ford's design and production experience and from access to its procurement and testing facilities. Consequently, build quality took a massive leap forward from earlier models and they are generally solid, well-built and reliable machines that can still give years of pleasure in everyday use. If you decide to buy one, it is my aim to see that you buy the best for your budget and avoid getting landed with a 'lemon'.

These cars sold very well over a long period and were largely responsible for countering Jaguar's previous reputation for unreliability (though that was never fully deserved). Large numbers were sold, many are still around, and this book aims to help you pick the best by being user-friendly, small enough to take with you to inspections, but detailed enough to help you check most aspects thoroughly. Be sure to look at several examples and enjoy your search!

Acknowledgements

I owe much to the X300/308 owners whose cooperation and help with photographs and information have been invaluable, in particular John Harwood, Andy Whalen, Shawn Amershek, Paul Dallas, Mike Stevens, Grahame Loader, Max Heazelwood, Ted Bacciarelli and Mark Krieger.

Peter Crespin
Cambridge

*(See the Veloce 1986-1994 XJ40 Buyer's Guide)

Contents

Essential Buyer's Guide™ currency
At the time of publication a BG unit of currency "●" equals approximately £1.00/
US$1.50/Euro 1.20. Please adjust to suit current exchange rates.

www.velocebooks.com / www.veloce.co.uk
All current books • New book news • Special offers • Gift vouchers

1 Is it the right car for you?
– marriage guidance!

Tall and short drivers
X300/308 front seats feature adjustable lumbar support and electric height adjustment. Many – including American models – have 12-way electric adjustment, including headrest height, plus seat/mirror position memory linked to the remote fobs. This is ideal for two-driver cars and includes entry/exit driver's seat and steering wheel retraction for improved access (albeit increasing motor wear). All steering wheels are reach/rake adjustable, electrically on electric seat cars. Thanks to squab height adjustment and lengthy seat runners, there is generous driver legroom. Headroom is good for tall drivers or average with a sunroof fitted.

Plenty of room for 5ft 10in Joe Hardy.

Weight of controls
X300/308 variable power steering is light when parking and firmer at speed. Most X300s were automatics, as were all X308s and all American cars of either type, but manuals have a moderately light clutch and good gear change – at a stretch. X300/308s have servo assisted ABS brakes which stop the car well. The handbrake isn't heavy but the angle was changed in 1995 to make reaching it easier, and it can press into thighs on low seat settings.

Tall Sarah Hardy with front seats back.

Will it fit the garage?
Length: 16ft 5.8in (5024mm)
Width (inc mirrors):   6ft 9.7in (2074mm)
Height: 4ft 3.7in (1314mm)

Interior space
The X300/308 is comfortable for five adults, although Daimler/Vanden Plas (VDP) deeply sculpted rear seats are better for two rear passengers (especially in long wheelbase cars with individually-reclining rear seats). Rear legroom is only adequate if the front seats are fully back, although long wheelbase rear legroom is generous. Rear headroom is also better for LWB back seat passengers, due to a raised roofline.

Luggage capacity
X300/308 boots are wide but slightly shallow; deepest in the models with a space-saver wheel and narrowest in models from '97 onwards with side-mounted CD player. The optional Harman Kardon amplifier and boot lid warning triangle intrude hardly at all,

12-way electric seats on top spec models.

if fitted. 1994/5 models had no glovebox but pockets on the front of the seats. The glovebox reduces passenger knee room fractionally. Doors have oddment bins and there's a console cubby box, plus rear cubby in cars with reclining rear seats. There are also magazine pockets behind the front seats and a toolbox under the bonnet, with tools on high-spec models.

Running costs

X300/308 are frugal for large luxury cars but still not cheap to run, with V8s slightly

better than the sixes, mostly because of the five-speed gearbox. 3.2L models are slightly better than 4.0L cars at (25-27mpg/ 24-26mpg) but gentle cruising in the higher-geared 4.0L cars often gives equal or better mileage due to higher gearing. The superchargers return 21-23mpg and smooth but heavy V12s, 18-20mpg. All figures depend on driving style and terrain but represent realistic averages (Imperial gallons). Being large cars, albeit all-alloy engines, they need to be driven for good distances to get hot – especially 1997-2000 Nikasil V8s – despite rapid warm-up features (see Chapter 7). Fuel price rises and taxation changes in some markets mean the value of these cars has fallen dramatically so initial costs can be very low.

Manual seats on base models.

Unless driven in harsh dusty or city environments, factory servicing intervals are 10,000 miles/12 months, being mostly fluid and filter checks/changes, plus plugs and gearbox, differential, brake and coolant fluids roughly every two years. Items such as ball and universal joints (even gearboxes and front wheel bearings on V8s) are sealed for life but repay checking and lubricant replacement. Many cars will have been serviced

Manual column adjust on early XJR6.

more often and a full service record is essential, especially for Nikasil V8s. The rubber suspension parts eventually wear and although the anti-roll bar and upper shock absorber and wishbone bushes are not expensive to replace, the lower wishbone and A-frame bushes cost more. DIY servicing and problem-solving is possible, especially on X300s, but the later the car the more likely specialist equipment will be needed.

Usability

X300/308s are very comfortable for long journey or daily driver roles, which are kinder to the car than short runs. All cars had automatic climate control but the earliest '94-'95 base model 3.2 cars lacked true refrigeration/air conditioning.

Parts availability

Jaguar dealerships obtain most parts from central depots, although some low-volume items (e.g.

CD intrudes into boot space on later cars.

clutches for manual XJRs) are no longer stocked. Alternative sources include independent Jaguar specialists or generic parts outlets. There is an increasing number of cars being dismantled for spares and several Jaguar specialists in this trade, such as Coventry West in America and EuroJag in the UK. Similar 6 and 12-cylinder engines were used in the last XJSs and the V8 debuted in the 1996 XK8 model, so many parts fit both. Some critical parts such as timing chain tensioners from later 4.2L V8s can be fitted to X308 cars.

Parts cost
Apart from basic service items, parts for these cars are reasonably expensive if you are used to low-budget mass market cars. Used parts can save a significant amount but it is wisest to invest in genuine Jaguar spares. Dealers can sometimes be remarkably competitive and are no worse than other prestige makes.

Insurance
Large luxury cars are not the cheapest to insure and these are too young to qualify for 'classic' insurance. Various Jaguar clubs have arranged good value insurance, sometimes with limited mileage, but if you are young or have a poor accident record it's wise to check insurance costs before buying.

Investment potential
X300/308s are not classics yet, like earlier Jaguars. The X300s are beginning to be more sought after, due to excellent reliability and user-friendly servicing compared to the V8s, but they are still cheap. Since these cars are at, or close to, the bottom of their value (especially early cars) there's an argument for buying now because their value is likely to increase over time. However, this is a gamble and only the very best low-mileage examples and some very rare models are likely to become collectable. Buy one of these cars to enjoy now, not in the hope of making gains in the future.

Alternatives
The X300/308 competed with cars such as BMW 7-Series, Mercedes S and E-class, Lexus 400 series and large luxury models from other makers. All suffer similar price falls and, in the case of BMW, their early V8s also had Nikasil problems. Buying a Jaguar is usually an emotive choice rather than the product of logic alone. If you're reading this it's probably because you have already decided Jaguars are still some of the world's most elegant cars, as well as quick and luxurious. In that case, a Lincoln, Cadillac or Lexus is unlikely to appeal.

2 Cost considerations
– affordable, or a money pit?

Purchase price
An average X300/308 costs the same as a used family car or newer small car. They are, therefore, fantastic value and, because of their size, are very safe. These are probably the best value Jaguars, with only the XJ40 being cheaper (but poorer value). As usual it's wise to buy the best you can afford, especially for main dealer history and lowish mileage. Apart from occasional trade-ins by loyal customers, the X300/X308s are no longer in official Jaguar dealers, though it's still worth asking if they know of any excellent cars locally. Most good cars are with independent Jaguar specialists, so scanning motor magazines will soon reveal which dealers concentrate on the type and price of car you require. Top dealers carry the best cars but at a price.

Make every trip a pleasure.

Jaguar club or specialist classic magazines (or web sites) are another source of good cars from knowledgeable sellers. Private sales vary from those asking foolishly high prices to realistic sellers wishing to dispose of a car that has served them well. To buy a good car privately this book or a knowledgeable friend will be useful to help avoid bad examples.

Affordable to run?
For X300/308s intended for regular use it is important to include fuel, servicing, consumables and insurance costs when deciding whether the car will be affordable. Modern cars depreciate but have low running costs and X300/308s are generally the opposite, apart from post 2000 V8s or rare sports, or special edition models which will still fall in value as their age and mileage

Angle hose to fill up faster.

increases. The X300 was, however, probably the most reliable Jaguar ever made until 2001, so although suspension and other parts will eventually wear, the basic reliability of the car will keep costs manageable.

Price bands
If you're looking at post-Nikasil Daimler/VDP or supercharged cars you can expect to pay up to £x10,000, or about half that for a 1997-2000 car (considerably less for an X300). At the time of writing, X300s are failing to sell on eBay at £x750. In the UK, new tax bands mean large post-2001 cars are being charged much higher rates, so excellent pre 2001 cars may benefit while post 2001 models drop in value.

Buy a wreck, build a good car?
There is no point paying for a project car or non-runner as there are too many good cars at low prices to make it worthwhile. The only exception might be an immaculate car in your perfect colour and specification, that has a sick V8 that you are confident of being able to fix or replace.

Servicing

Job	Interval
Basic oil change	5-10,000 miles
Routine service	10,000 miles or 12 months
Major service	30,000 miles or 3 yearly
Coolant, brake fluid changes, suspension bushes etc.	Coolant and brake fluid 2 yearly. Others as needed

Ultimate luxury – reclining electric seats.

X300/308 parts prices*
Mechanical parts

Part	X300 Jaguar	Aftermarket	X308 Jaguar	Aftermarket
Brake pads front	55	26	55	18
Brake pads rear	41	18	34	18
Head gasket set	80	45	166	127
Fuel pump	248	103	91	49
Radiator	236	N/A	236	N/A
Alternator	286	139	286	140
Water pump	195	112	42	63
Shock abs front	108	47	95	105
Shock abs rear	97	63	101	66
Starter motor	196	65	234	161
Air con condenser	408	82	408	82
Receiver/drier	53	29	44	39
Wheel bearings FR	29	14	35	14

Wheel bearings R	29	19	15	13
Front hub assy	103	67	103	67
Rear hub assy	103	81	103	81
Steering rack	1331	243	1183	N/A

Prices exclude UK tax (not payable on export orders). Courtesy SNG Barratt Ltd.

Used parts
These are plentiful – check literature for dealers
eBay tends to list fewer spare parts for X300/308s than it does for more valuable classics, but you can see which Jaguar dismantlers operate in your market. See also Owner's Club classifieds, autojumbles/swapmeets.

Trying Dad's car. A safe vehicle for all the family.

www.velocebooks.com / www.veloce.co.uk
All current books • New book news • Special offers • Gift vouchers

3 Living with an XJ
– will you get along together?

Good points
Superb refinement and comfort.
Good handling and grip for a large luxury car.
Powerful engines, smooth transmissions.
Elegant lines and road presence.
Well-equipped with most creature comforts.
Smooth power and performance, with great refinement.
Full instrumentation and lots of extras if required.
Safe and strong vehicle for family use.
Good corrosion protection and all-round durability.
6-cylinder cars can be serviced at home.
A range of models and prices.

First Class Express – the XJR6.

Tools almost never needed.

Bad points
V8 bore, water pump and timing chain reliability pre-2000.
V8 timing chain problems even post-2000.
V8 transmission reliability at high mileage if oil unchanged.
Fuel consumption, especially V12 and superchargers.
Differential weep or output shaft play.
X300 fascia clock digits and heater pump brushes can fail.
Stone damage to AC condenser or compressor seal failure.
Cost of V12 engine work and some specialist parts.
Complex suspension often requires refurbishment.
Rear arch and radiator support corrosion in early cars.
Occasional sticking throttle/stalling.

Summary
A superbly handsome and refined car, blighted by some engine reliability problems on early V8s, but many have been repaired by now. A good one is a truly great car. Electrically and mechanically almost trouble free in other respects. High mileage cars may need some suspension refurbishment but serious body corrosion is rare. Cooling system needs flushing and maintenance and brake fluid should be changed to keep the ABS system working correctly. A good one should run long and strong and win you over very quickly. A car for the heart AND the head.

Gus Glikas' pride and joy.

Models

There are many X300/308 models but, apart from the 3.2 and manual models (not imported to America/Canada), price depends more on condition and specification. In most markets there are five engines plus two supercharged versions, three main trim levels (XJ, Sovereign and Daimler/Vanden Plas) plus Sport and limited editions.

Sporting, comfortable long-legged XJR.

If you are new to Jaguars a base model may well offer the refinement and toys you need at a lower price and running cost compared to a higher spec or larger model. The best option depends on intended use. A 3.2 is not slow, and there are plenty of Sovereigns and Sport models this size, offering cheaper insurance. Daimlers were all 4.0L, and the best value and resale option is a Sovereign or Daimler/VDP. The XJR6 and XJR8 are popular with sporting drivers, and Double Sixes or Super V8s combine fast engines with luxurious trim, albeit with softer handling than an XJR.

At home on the byways too.

X300s are classic Jaguars inside, with six dials in a typical cluster and straight dash and door wood trim. The V8s have curvy dashboards and door wood and lost two instruments, but they do have other options, such as rain sensing wipers. Some long wheelbase models have separate reclining rear seats – the pinnacle of Jaguar/Daimler luxury at the time and are still first class today.

The later the car, the lower the risk of body and suspension deterioration but few are seriously rusty. All enjoyed far better build and component quality than earlier Jaguars. The sporting X300/308s are better drivers' cars, but the 'touring' models handle well enough. Jaguar's 'CATS' suspension rides softly until speed and cornering forces increase, whereupon the dampers firm up.

Jaguar used the Vanden Plas name rather than Daimler in North America for top of the range models. These were 'fully loaded' with most accessories, and often the premium Harman Kardon stereo system, heated seats and screens, etc. They feature chromed door handles, mirror backs and rubbing strips, with boxwood inlaid veneers and full leather trim, rather than part leather.

Values

Due to the many variations available these are approximate values only. The dearest models are rated at 100% and others shown as a percentage of that value. Note, however, that the price for a given model depends more on condition than its notional value in this table. A highly-specified car will always sell for more, or more quickly, than a base model.

V12 the old smoothie. Anything else is less.

Supercharged cars are worth more but some buyers are put off by running costs or perceived added complexity. The V12 models are most cost-sensitive, however, and although these last V12s are super-reliable, they're inevitably more complex and thirstier.

The dearest cars originally will fall by the most and the base cars will sell slowest, so mid-range models are the most firmly priced. Avoid hard-used worn examples with mega-mileages, but don't be afraid of well-serviced and clean cars showing, say, 150,000 miles. A good one has many years of life left in it yet.

When new, automatic transmission cost extra and manual transmissions were the base specification. Today, because of rarity and fuel economy benefits, manuals sometimes cost slightly more. All values vary according to condition and market.

No A/C and manual gear-change. Base model 3.2 Sport.

2001/2 XJR100 Limited Edition	**100%**
2001-2003 Daimler/VDP Super V8	**95%**
2001-2003 XJR8	**90%**
2001-2003 Sovereign V8	**80%**
1996 Daimler Century Special Edition	**80%**
1994-1997 XJR6	**75%**
1994-1996 V12 Daimler Double Six/Jaguar XJ12	**70%**
2001-2003 XJ8	**65%**
1994-1997 Daimler Six	**60%**
1997-2000 Sovereign V8	**50%**
1994-1997 Sovereign	**45%**
1997-2000 XJ8	**45%**
1994-1997 XJ6/XJ Sport	**40%**

5 Before you view
– be well informed

The X300/308 revived Jaguar's fortunes and put it above some German and Japanese makes in customer surveys. They are excellent cars and can still look almost new a decade later. They were made in large numbers apart from models such as Daimler Double Sixes or XJ12s. You therefore have plenty of choice, even restricting your search to good cars at a wide range of prices. Unless you have special reasons, avoid buying a project or scruffy car and save your inspections for good candidates. Sift these carefully by phone beforehand, since sellers can get carried away in advertisements and give 'optimistic' descriptions.

Glass in vent. A write-off, maybe?

Ask direct specific questions, not general enquiries such as whether the car is 'good'. Ask instead if the rear wheelarches are rusty, or the jacking points or screen surrounds. Are the sills good and the bottoms of the doors and the roof around the sunroof aperture? Does the boot leak, or the suspension rattle over bumps? If the seller says there is no wear on the driver's seat are they

View at home or business premises.

really sure their car is perfect? They may admit to some scuffs or minor body rust, which opens up the discussion. Few sellers will misrepresent a car when questioned directly. The credibility and attitude of the seller will hopefully become apparent during such questioning, which nobody reasonable should object to.

Body rust is not the major problem that it was on earlier Jaguars, although it needs checking. Instead, on V8s cylinder bores, timing gear and water pump are weak points and the gearbox on all cars has to be looked after, so ask about these areas. On the earlier sixes ask if there are any oil leaks from the front of the engine or anywhere on the transmission. In all cases ask about wheel bearing noise or suspension clonking. Ask if every single window, lock, switch and control works properly and if the air conditioning blows cold. For V8s, ask if a replacement engine or gearbox has ever been fitted.

Where is the car?
You should find plenty of standard models in your area but may need to look further

afield for rare models like Double Sixes or Super V8s. If buying from a specialist dealer, even long distance, you should be able to get an excellent picture of the car from a telephone conversation and emailed photos. Try to avoid cars from salted road or maritime areas, unless they have been winter stored – the X300/308 has lots of zinc-coated steel but is not rustproof. After the '96 model year the rear arch underseal was improved and these cars are usually solid.

Dealer or private sale?

A good dealer should only offer solid cars for resale, although Jaguar club advertisements also contain many

Two fewer gauges – the V8 dashboard.

good private sales. Not surprisingly, the more you pay the better the car – especially from long-established Jaguar specialists with reputations to protect. The cars are past the point where Jaguar offered replacement engines for early V8s, and electrical or transmission gremlins can strike at any time, so warranties from dealers can be useful.

Dealers usually also offer finance, which is another good reason for using them for higher-priced cars. However, if you need finance just to buy the car, check that your budget can stretch to likely repair, service and fuel costs.

The dealers buy and sell through trade auctions and you can do the same (see Chapter 10). Often you'll find superb value privately, especially from long-term owners or fellow enthusiasts who have looked after the car with pride.

The mighty V12.

Ask sellers about service history and paperwork. Good ownership involves significant maintenance, so there should be either receipts for parts or bills from a service establishment.

Viewing arrangements

Avoid viewing at the roadside or a car park if possible and try to view at the seller's business or private home

Ask about body damage.

(a private seller's name and address should be the same as on the title document). View at least once in daylight and in dry weather, to detect paint and body flaws. If you have to view in wet weather, use the opportunity to check for screen or boot leaks.

Reason for sale

Good sellers always explain why they are selling, even if it's just for a cheaper car. If this is the reason, be careful to check for shortcuts in servicing records. Avoid cars with an inspection certificate which is about to expire as the owner may have just discovered problems needing fixing to pass and decide to sell instead. Some inspection authorities, such as VOSA in the UK, permit on-line viewing of the reasons for failure, as well as the advisory notices issued at the last test, even if the car passed.

Upgraded to 18in Pentas.

Originality
These relatively new cars are usually in totally original specification, apart from minor changes such as wheels or exhausts, etc. Originality is desirable for ease of servicing and trouble-shooting as X300/308s are complex cars and deviations from standard can introduce problems. An upgraded stereo, or Jaguar additions such as a half-wood steering wheel or cup-holder are fine, but lowered suspension, ultra low-profile tyres or heavily tinted windows can lower value.

Very occasionally a normally-aspirated X300/308 can be tuned or given the supercharged engine from an XJR or Super V8. Be sceptical of the quality of work, as it is more cost-effective to buy a supercharged car in the first place. The cost of conversion is higher than the difference in price between normally-aspirated and forced induction.

Matching data/legal ownership
The X300/308 has a modern Vehicle Identification Number (VIN) visible through the screen on a tab, and stamped on the front bulkhead seam, so checking the car versus documentation is easy.

Does the vendor own the car outright or is money owed on it or is it even stolen? Finance checks can often also confirm if the car has ever been a write-off.

Inside-out sill corrosion.

In the UK the following organisations supply vehicle data –
HPI – 01722 422 422
AA – 0870 600 0836
DVLA – 0870 240 0010
RAC – 0870 533 3660
Other countries will have similar organisations.

Roadworthiness
Does the car have a roadworthiness or emissions certificate? Test status for UK cars can be checked on 0845 600 5977. Similar checks are available in some other markets. North American cars are no longer divided into California or other states and all share common emissions equipment.

Unleaded fuel
All X300/308s use unleaded fuel and have knock sensors that automatically retard the ignition if detonation is encountered. This keeps the engine safe but reduces power and economy, so use the recommended fuel for your market.

Payment
A cheque takes time to clear and sellers may prefer a cash buyer. Cash can be a valuable bargaining tool but a banker's draft or money order may be acceptable, so ask beforehand.

Buying at auction?
See Chapter 10.

Professional vehicle check
X300/308s are complex, refined fast cars and need to be fully roadworthy for use in modern high-speed traffic. Your local motoring organisation or marque/model specialist will usually conduct a professional examination for a fee. For V12s, try to perform, or pay for, a full compression check. One or two poor cylinders can be missed, even on a road test, if you are unfamiliar with V12s. On older V8s ask for a blow-by check.

Other organisations providing car checks in the UK are –
AA – 0800 085 3007 (motoring organisation with vehicle inspectors)
ABS – 0800 358 5855 (specialist vehicle inspectors)
RAC – 0870 533 3660 (motoring organisation with vehicle inspectors)
Other countries will have similar services.

Rain or heavy dew spoils paint inspection.

6 Inspection equipment
– these items will really help

The X300/308 models were the first Jaguars equipped with full on-board diagnostics (OBD) rather than a vehicle monitoring computer or nothing. The system is industry standard OBD2 (OBDII) and simple code readers are available for around ●35, less in the USA. Computer-based scanners cost more, but at least a small code reader is worthwhile since it will be useful during your ownership if you buy, as well as during inspection. Read the instructions and find the OBD2 port which looks like a SCART socket between the steering column and the centre console under the dashboard. See www.jag-lovers.org for a code list or check the scanner booklet. The climate control system also has a self-test facility (see Chapter 9).

Axle stands and jack are useful.

The most important inspection tools are your senses so bring a good torch and inspect the car at least once in daylight or excellent artificial light. X300/308s don't leak much but may have been flooded, so look and smell for damp and mould around foot wells and in the boot, although damp can arise from blocked air conditioner drains. Touch helps you discover poor welded arch repairs and botched filler patches. Besides the torch and scanner you will need:

This book
Trolley jack(s) and stands
Small mirror on a stick
Probe or small screwdriver
Digital camera
Scanner code list
Long probe or mechanic's stethoscope
A knowledgeable friend

Vital tool – an OBD2 scanner.

Useful extras: Compression gauge with long connector (especially for V12s), antifreeze concentration hydrometer, test strips for checking combustion products in coolant (head gasket leak), IR thermometer for checking misfiring cylinders.

There should be no filler on a modern Jaguar, but take a small magnet just in case. The camera is handy to compare cars later if reviewing more than one inspection, or to get feedback from others.

On these models 60% of the body is made of steel coated with zinc. Whilst not

Use your hands too.

as effective as hot-dip galvanising, this, together with effective seam sealing/cavity waxing, means the cars are lasting well. Consequently, surface corrosion may be all there is though there are plenty of cars with none at all, so avoid questionable examples. Significant filler or poor bodywork should rule out the car.

A small screwdriver can be used – with care – as a probe, particularly on the inner and outer sills, chassis sections over the A-frame front mounts, and the front of the footwells. The frame under the radiator is often corroded but not accessible if the undertray is still in place.

Some faults can't be hidden.

The stick mirror helps check the underside, around the manifolds if the exhaust is blowing, or for seepage from a coolant hose underneath the inlet manifold. A ramp inspection is obviously ideal, but two trolley jacks plus axle stands can provide viewing room for one side or one end at a time.

There are no high-tension leads or distributor on any X300/X308 except the V12 (which, though distributor-less, still has short leads from its coil packs). A code reader is the easiest way to check current and recent engine function.

If possible, use a test strip to check for the right type and strength of coolant. Ideally you'll also be able to check for signs of combustion gases from a faulty head gasket, especially if there's bubbling or exhaust smells. If no blow-by test is available for a V8 and there is no sign of a replacement engine having been fitted in a pre-2000 car, be careful and do not pay top money. A replacement engine can be identified by the green ID label on the block at the back of the right side cylinder head and, of course, by looking at the service record.

www.velocebooks.com / www.veloce.co.uk
All current books • New book news • Special offers • Gift vouchers

7 Fifteen minute evaluation
– walk away or stay?

Road test

Any X300/X308 should impress on road test, but for a pre-2001 V8 ask the owner not to start the car before you arrive to check cold starting and possible emerging Nikasil issues. A rattle on cold start-up that disappears almost instantly is acceptable, but if it continues for some seconds it indicates timing chain trouble, more serious on V8s than sixes. A V12 should rustle quietly more or less immediately. For private sales take care not to switch off until it has at least warmed for a few minutes, in case you provoke a known fuelling glitch which can flood the engine. This is mostly just embarrassing on sixes (which usually start after prolonged cranking with the pedal held to the floor). Doing this at a dealer's premises is less problematic, as you can walk away if needs be, but flooding can damage V8s or cause a serious no-start requiring oil in the bores to get it going.

The road test is vital.

Check in the mirror if you are driving, or look behind if being driven, there should be no smoke even on first start-up. Vapour clouds are normal in chilly weather, provided they clear once underway. While at it, check the mirror itself to see if it's an auto-dimmer, as these can leak corrosive chemicals on the console. If it is, put your finger over the day/night sensor at the front and see if the glass darkens.

X300s are well insulated from engine and road noise and X308s even more so, due to a shorter engine and type of double bulkhead. There should be little or no wind

Make sure you are insured!

noise and the car should impress with its smoothness and excellent ride control with no wallowing. Apart from a slight permissible clunk when selecting reverse from drive (or vice versa), there should be no transmission noise. Very faint axle whine is permissible but anything clearly audible spells trouble.

Sports models ride on firmer springs/dampers and lower profile tyres but are still supple and smooth. As in any other car, a whine related to road speed, that alters in turns, hints at wheel bearing trouble. Whilst these are easy to repair on a six or twelve, the V8 design needs special tools and a press. Anything that feels or sounds like

Dust is OK. Dirty oil is not.

The usual view other drivers get of these cars.

Very common clock problem.

looseness or scraping indicates work is needed – ranging from a worn ball or universal joint to damper bushes. If the car skips sideways on bumps in bends, suspect worn A-frame bushes. A light rattle from the front right footwell area on a six could be the catalytic converter heat shield splitting, whereas blowing is the downpipes themselves or their joint with the main exhaust system. Exhaust manifolds are known to crack, especially on sixes, so listen carefully.

Any X300/308 should accelerate strongly/very strongly, depending on engine. There should be no smoke under acceleration once warm, or on the overrun, when puffs of blue indicate worn guide seals or rings. All engines should be smooth, although the sixes are coarser than the V8s and, of course, the V12s. Even the V12 becomes raucous when revved to red line, however. A whistling noise from the XJR supercharger is normal.

Try all windows and mirrors and other controls, such as cruise control. Brake firmly on a quiet road to check for warning lights, noises or juddering. Brakes should be powerful and progressive and not pull sideways, even with hands-free steering (except for a mild camber effect). Mild vibration at speed can be tyre or drive shaft imbalance, but juddering indicates warped or corroded discs and/or suspension problems. Excessive bouncing indicates worn dampers that are sometimes also audible when bouncing the car at each corner. Make several low speed, full-lock turns to check for wheel rubbing or power steering noises, especially if non-standard wheels/tyres are fitted. V12s or sport models with PowrLok limited slip differentials may creak from the rear at full lock.

The handbrake is usually fine but check for hold and release.

Check all the instruments, although the oil pressure dial on most models is just a mid-dial 'on/off' indicator, not an analogue gauge. Temperature should stay steady in the middle, and the voltmeter just to the right of centre to indicate charge. The four-speed automatic gearbox of the 3.2 six is smooth, and the electronic 4.0L six box is even better, as is the slightly different box on V12 and XJR6 cars. Smoothest of all are the five-speeds on the V8s. Manual gearboxes on the sixes should be silent in all ratios, and depressing the clutch should not cause any screeching, though faint release bearing noises can occur.

Try the air conditioning to check it blows colder than ambient.

Checks back at base

If all seems well you're ready delve deeper. When the engine and transmission are fully warm, move the auto selector through all positions 2-3 times and leave the engine idling while you pull the dipstick and clean/re-insert to check the fluid level is between the hot markings. If the fluid is brown instead of red, or smells burnt, this shows lack of maintenance. Look for oil leakage on sixes near the cam position sensor (front right of engine). Check for cam cover leakage on sixes or magnesium crumbling around the edges. Whilst under the bonnet, set the air conditioning to maximum cold and listen for a rumbling compressor bearing. The supercharger bearings are also audible when worn, as are steering pump, alternator or idler pulleys.

Check filler recess drain.

General condition

X300/308s inspire pride of ownership and are still new enough that they should not have been neglected or show signs of careless use. Such cars should be avoided unless you're certain the grubbiness is only skin deep. Any car that looks immaculate has probably (but not invariably) been also well-treated mechanically.

Body and interior

Are the carpets clean and the leather supple and unmarked? Base models have half cloth upholstery but all suffer from abrasive wear on the driver's outer bolster. Are the armrests clean and un-cracked, the door panels firmly attached and the veneer unmarked, with the under-dash panels firmly in place? The centre console tends to bleach first and there was a short run of cars around 2000 where the lacquer went milky (most have been replaced under warranty).

Test every single switch.

Are the boot lid lining and triangle properly attached? Is the boot floor clean and the spare in good condition with the boot floor unrusted? Are there signs of damp or leaks from the boot lid or fuel filler? Is the electric aerial jammed or the aerial grommet split?

Are panel gaps good with no door drop – especially on the driver's

Check safety and spare kit.

door? Is there rust bubbling around the screens or traces of water damage inside? Headlinings drop less than earlier Jaguars but it still happens, especially at the front and rear curves and roof console. Check that the sunroof tilts and retracts smoothly.

Investigate musty leak smells.

Tyre wear or suspension trouble?

X300/308 rustproofing was good but water can get behind the front wings or creep behind the black sealant under the body floor. The jacking points especially can bend or rot, as can the rear bumper hangers each side. Try to see as much of the underside as possible – ideally on a lift. The underseal is coming to the end of its life now and can flake off.

Sills should be good but check for accident damage and rust at each end and along the lower inside seam with the floor. Check the footwells by lifting the carpets to view. Does the bonnet hold itself open and look rust and dent free from inside? They are much better than earlier models.

Rear vent is often kicked and damaged.

Does the car sit right, with no corner lower than any other? Pull the wheels to and fro hard at the top as a preliminary check for slack bearings or worn suspension/ drive universals or differential output bearings. Have the owner turn the steering while you view the steering ball joints and rack body for movement. Look at tyres for unusual wear, indicating suspension or alignment problems. Look for split or crumbling suspension bushes at all pivots or attachment points, especially the A-frame bushes and upper front damper mounts. Small stones jammed in the bushes can lead to odd interior rattles. Check for leaks from the differential input and output seals. Oil mist around the differential breather is normal.

Dry differential – a good sign.

8 Key points

– where to look for problems

Key aspects to check on X300/308s are:

Engine condition
Transmission, suspension and brakes
Instruments and electrics
Interior trim
Structural bodywork

Engines

The 6-cylinder engines are very strong, having been designed initially to permit a diesel version. Apart from an oil leak at the front right corner, or early timing chain tensioner troubles, they are practically bomb proof. The 6.0L V12 is also very strong, though neither like overheating and V12

Lionheart: unburstable AJ16 engine.

throttle linkage bushes wear. If they sound good they probably are good, although the block water hose and exhaust manifolds can leak.

The later V8s are good too, but there are issues with the early versions (engine number below 0008181043). Before 2000 when high-sulphur fuel was common, cars used for short cold trips could damage the Nikasil bore lining, leading to lost compression, poor starting and engine replacement. Meanwhile, three types of chain tensioner were tried before the final all-metal version was used on 4.2 V8s. A failed tensioner can cause timing chain snap, or skip, and bend the valves on the affected bank. The early water pumps with plastic vanes were also prone to break up and pieces could lodge in waterways to cause overheating, even after replacement. The thermostat housing can also crack and top hoses blow off. Any sign of clattering means tensioner trouble and urgent repairs. There should be no coolant leaks or white powdery deposits from former seepage. Throttle bodies and linkages should be clean with unworn bushes.

Transmission, suspension and brakes

The sixes use dependable 4-speed ZF automatics, electronic mode-selectable on the 4.0L cars, with a strong GM truck type on the XJR and also V12. Manual sixes use a strong Getrag. All X300s should have fluid and filter changes in their service records every 60,000 miles maximum. The V8s use 'sealed for life' transmissions but these suffer eventually if the fluid is not

ABS multiplug sometimes corrodes.

changed. Check records carefully and examine fluid level and colour. Apart from fluid checks when hot it is mostly only possible to check for smooth gear selection and listen for excessive whine or knocks on hard acceleration, harsh shifting, slipping clutches or to/fro clunking of loose mountings.

The strong differential is normally good even if seals need replacing but the rubber Jurid propshaft coupling can crack and split. If the output shafts are loose this will be obvious by pulling-pushing the top of the rear wheels even without jacking the car up. The suspension's many rubber/foam bushings will eventually wear and lead to knocking noises over bumps.

The brakes are sturdy and dependable unless the hand brake has been left on (which burns the shoes). In salt road areas, suspect sticking pins or caliper pistons if the brakes pull unevenly. Cars with CATS suspension should ride differently under fast or slow conditions. Apart from track rod ends on sixes and twelves and front wheel bearings, most suspension repairs need some expertise or special tools to fix.

Instruments and electrics

The electrics and instruments are reliable, but are complex and potentially expensive to fix so check them by working methodically through all the car's systems and controls. The full engine management systems controlling fuel and ignition and faults are monitored via on-board diagnostics and many problems are due to loose connections, such as the ABS pump or earth studs on the bulkhead or chassis. The left-hand rear ABS wheel sensor can affect the ABS and traction control. The mirror adjustment switch can break and windows or electric roof become sluggish, but other parts are durable.

Early lamp modules can fail.

Interiors

The interiors are very hardwearing, whether leather or sports fabric. The door panels come loose if not properly refitted after working behind them, and the driver's seat frame can break or the bolster deteriorate, as does the driver's side of the console armrest. Most of the rest should be excellent. Headlinings can sag on early cars and veneer crack or lift but both are much rarer than previous Jaguars. Check for musty smells from water leaks and sickly sweet smells from leaked coolant or hydraulic fluids.

Tough but neglected interior.

Bodywork

X300/308 cars are all monocoque (frameless) construction so many rust areas could affect the integrity of the structure directly or indirectly. Thankfully, there are very few rust areas and most of those are obvious around the wheelarches and wings front and rear. The radiator support is often corroded and is hard to examine, but it's not expensive to replace the bolt-on piece.

The X300/308 has bonded screens, although the plastic seals can allow water to collect and rust around the base or even upper edges where the steel was not zinc coated. It is much rarer than previous Jaguars but not unheard of, so look carefully. The old XJ40 bonnet and boot rust traps practically never occur on the X300/X308.

Two tensioner-damaged engines.

www.velocebooks.com / www.veloce.co.uk
All current books • New book news • Special offers • Gift vouchers

9 Serious evaluation
– 60 minutes for years of enjoyment

So, you've narrowed it down to a full inspection candidate to decide on purchase and price. Tick the appropriate box for each check and total the points. Be realistic where bodywork is concerned and vigilant for V8 engine faults.

Overall stance

Ex 4 Gd 3 Av 2 Po 1

All the late XJs should sit flat or slightly tail-high, especially with an empty boot and low fuel load (check the gauge). The distance from the ground to the centre of each wheelarch should be around 27in/660mm and anything much below 26in/635mm indicates sagging suspension, depending on tyre profile (60 series versus 55 on 16in wheels). The XJRs and Sport models sit slightly lower all round and the heavy V12 is often sagging by now, sometimes at both ends, making it level, but low. The car should sit level when viewed from front or back.

Shawn Amershek's dead level car.

Bodywork panels

Ex 4 Gd 3 Av 2 Po 1

Good X300/308s have undistorted panels with even shut lines and few or no car park dents. Look for even gaps between bumpers and body and that the ends line up with the wheelarches. Bumper mounts can corrode and the covers drop off entirely. Look for bubbling halfway along the bottom edge of the rear wing where the hanger attaches. Even slight warping on X300

Reflections help assess panel lines.

27

bumper chrome indicates parking damage and likely beam damage behind. Lighter X308 plastic covers show kinks and damage easily.

Feel inside the wheelarches for rough metal or double thickness from repairs, especially in the rear arches and lower rear area of the front wings. Loose or missing mud shields in the front wheelarch can hide rot or leave brake cooling ducts hanging, so clean and inspect by torchlight. Check the front undertray and brake cooling ducts are

Arches replaced, double hidden edge.

present, and that no temperature sensor wires dangle free. The area around the filler flap can suffer badly and the radiator support crossmember often corrodes but is hard to see with the undertray in place.

Underside, sills and floors

Ex	Gd	Av	Po
4	3	2	1

The front footwell corners around the jacking points can rust if the underseal has been damaged. The open jacking points can be the start of rust here. If there's any footwell rust pull the carpets back if possible to check for internal corrosion. Look

inside the rear wings over the silencers and feel and push the bumper side bracket to check corrosion. If you have time, try to lift the car at each jack point to look for body weakness. Other weld areas are around the A-frame mounts or sill seams. Beware thick underseal over poor welding or bad steel. The A-frame can look rusty but is usually not dangerously rotten and is replaceable. Look for rotten rubber or collapsed A-frame bushes just ahead of each rear wheel. Look inside the rear door apertures for rot from inside the sills at the back. The front upper section of the sills

Good intact underseal.

is hidden behind the wings, but water and mud can collect here behind the splash panel and rot down from above.

Bonnet, inner wings and boot

Ex	Gd	Av	Po
4	3	2	1

These are all better than earlier Jaguars, with corrosion rare. There can be rust where a boot or bonnet has hit the body repeatedly on closing. The inner front wings are usually sound but at the back of the engine compartment the bulkhead can rust from inside out or cause cabin leaks if plenum drains are blocked with leaves, so check carefully behind the brake servo and opposite side. The seam under the rear bonnet seal often hides rust from the clips damaging the paint. Look for accident repairs, rippling on the main chassis rails (although they do have 'notch-like'

Bonnet rust is very rare.

crumple zone depressions every few inches). Top shock absorber mounts can be checked, at least on the side away from the header tank.

While checking the boot lid see if the boot lights illuminate and the electric push button lock works (and the key lock). The harness taped to the right boot hinge often cracks, and one or other electrical boot lid function fails. Peep behind the number plate if possible to look for holes cut in the panel to open a stuck boot. Electrical components in the boot hate damp so look under the trims for rust or damaged wiring/fuses.

Doors

Ex Gd Av Po
4 3 2 1

Check the door gaps and feel along the corners and bottom edges. Door latch cables can break so check all, inside and out. Check the courtesy light delay operates and there is no rapid flickering, indicating

Boot hinge harness can crack.

Check for bulkhead rust.

a sticking latch microswitch, often in a rear door. Check all windows and all doors lock centrally. Remember there is a child lock on the rears so if they do not open see if it is activated. Door drop normally only affects the driver's door, so lift it and look for heavy strike marks on the latch components, as well as a loose/damaged door card or armrest. Doors should fit flush and thud closed, not clang. The rubber body to door harness sleeves perish and let water into the door casing so see the drains are free. Perimeter seals should be intact and not broken or worn on the top where they catch clothing.

Fuel tank and pipework

Ex Gd Av Po
4 3 2 1

Fuel tanks are usually fine inside the dry boot, but check for fuel smells and a filler recess drain blocked with leaf debris or split from age. Look for signs to indicate the boot trim has been disturbed during remedial work of some sort. It is often replaced shoddily, and in the wrong order, leaving unsightly seams or oily finger prints. Front boot trim panel removal suggests fuel tank repairs or pump trouble. Right trim damage suggests ECU or electric aerial problems, and left cover damage suggests fuel filler solenoid issues

Boot lid button can break.

Boot lid cut to free stuck lock.

or leakage problems. If not already done, lift the right floor panel to check the correct long battery is present, not a cheaper but wrong smaller battery. Examine the spare tyre for heavy or uneven wear, suggesting suspension bush or alignment issues. Are the jack and tools under the spare, including two neat chocks? Just in front of the left rear wheel is the fuel filter. Does it look recent and the alloy pipes uncorroded?

Exposed fuel pipes can corrode.

Sunroof

Check for rust around the sunroof opening, either at the edges or for spidery rust spreading under the paint from stonechips. Check the roof opens smoothly without juddering and closes correctly. Look for light fresh grease rather than hard stiff caked material. Headliner stains suggest blocked drains or a poor seal, which can be covered in moss and break up.

Paint

Metallic paints are most common and not the hardest formula. Consequently there are normally stonechips around the grille, headlights and leading edges of all wheelarch flares. For darker colours these are more obvious since the undercoat is a pale colour, but in all cases look for signs of rust beginning and previous touch-up work. The X300/308 was a valuable car, so expect signs of careful paint touch up and possibly panel re-sprays - not necessarily for accident damage but to revive the finish on

Soft paint stonechips easily.

a quality car. Look for spray work around the wheelarches, filler flap and screen base. Check for overspray inside wheelarches or on rubber aperture seals and cable sheaths into doors. Look for poor finish inside the fuel filler and the tops of the inner wings. See Chapter 14.

Lights & body trim

The X300 had twin-bulb front turn signals and twin rear lamps. Both reverted to single lamps on X308. Check the headlamp glasses for stone chips or sand blasting from high mileage road debris. Greyish deposits inside can sometimes be cleaned from inside with alcohol swabs but the X308 'jewel' headlamps should be bright and clear. Front fog lamps are often damaged so check they work. Various earth studs are used by the lights and indicators so see all lamps work correctly and if more than one is out it may be an earth problem. The lights are controlled by expensive lamp modules so failures should be treated with caution, whether the bulb fail warning light is on or off.

Even plastic chrome can flake.

The long bright trims on each bumper are easy to bend with parking contact and short V8 ones can split as they are chromed plastic, not stainless. Even if trims and bumper seem intact, look underneath to see if they're secured to the beam firmly as beams may split or bend.

Is the body colour rubbing strip securely

Corroded mounts let bumper hang.

fixed all round and any extra chrome strips on Daimler VDP models likewise secure? Mirror covers can crack from being struck, including chrome Daimler VDP ones (which are vacuum-plated plastic).

Stainless window trims usually survive well but many boot badges begin to bubble under the plastic outer layer after some years.

Body seals

Ex	Gd	Av	Po
4	3	2	1

The X300/308 was the most refined Jaguar to that time, due to good bulkhead and door aperture sealing, amongst other factors. Furflex door aperture trim is largely decorative, but often shows dark streaks from air leaks. See the soft rubber door surround is undamaged and boot and bonnet seals intact. Screen seals are critical, even though the glass itself is bonded, and rust bubbles can appear at the top, sides, or base of the screen.

Rust under bonnet rear seal.

Wheels and tyres

Ex	Gd	Av	Po
4	3	2	1

Most X300/308s were supplied with 16 x 7in wheels, steel on base models (where sold). The V12 and some Sports models used 16 x 8in rims and lower profile tyres, with the XJR on Jaguar's biggest-ever wheel at 17in, later to become the 18in Penta on XJR8. Look for inevitable oxidation damage under the lacquer, especially on diamond cut wheels which are expensive to refurbish except by painting instead of re-cutting. Steel wheels used full plastic trims which are more expensive to buy new than a used set of alloys, so many cars have been upgraded. Wheels from a later 1997-2003 X308 can make an X300 look younger. The choice of tyre and wheels is a

Typical wheel corrosion.

compromise between comfort and sharp handling but standard sizes are good. The tyres are expensive so check that there is a good make fitted, preferably all four the same with plenty of tread left. Look for unusual wear on the inner or outer edges, suggesting either poor alignment or suspension trouble.

Exhaust

Ex	Gd	Av	Po
4	3	2	1

All X300/308 cars used twin exhausts with characteristic oval rolled-edge trims, apart from V8 supercharged models' larger round trims. The system is expensive, with four catalysts on all cars and either two or four oxygen sensors. Middle catalyst substitute pipes are a cost-effective alternative to expensive replacements and the car should still pass emissions. The downpipe on sixes can split near the back inside the heat shield but this can normally be TIG welded to save replacing the whole twin-catalyst piece. The heat shield can also partly detach, giving a

Catalyst replacement pipes.

buzzing vibration. V8 and V12 systems are symmetrical from the start and give little trouble for at least ten years. The centre rear hanger

AJ16 heat shields can rattle or split.

rubber is often split or missing, which puts more strain on the rest, so shake the pipework when cooled to see it is securely attached. The thin

V8 manifolds rarely crack.

cast-iron manifolds can crack and give a characteristic blowing sound under the sheet metal shields. Hissing or blowing noises which would indicate a failed gasket or stripped studs – especially awkward on all V engines.

Glass and wipers

Ex	Gd	Av	Po
4	3	2	1

The large single wiper travels fast across the screen, and tends to cloud the glass with an arc of very fine scratches. The system ensures little lift at speed and the increased faint scratching is a nuisance; dealers were supposed to polish the screen with special paste every service, but it can be years since this was done. V8s have washer jets mounted on the blade and usually an auto wiper system. Heated front screens use twin elements and relays and may fail on one or both sides due to switch, wire or relay problems. The rear heated screen is robust unless heavy objects that

V8 wiper carries washer jets.

are carried on the parcel shelf knock and damage the element or its contacts.

Switch gear is robust but check that the intermittent wash-wipe works.

Rear suspension & brakes

Ex	Gd	Av	Po
4	3	2	1

The X300/308 used a similar system to the XJ40, which isolates the occupants very well from road shocks and noise. It allows significant fore and aft movement of the wheels which, in turn, needed specialised shock absorbers; some early Boge aftermarket shocks were not suitable and broke. Complete inspection requires wheel removal, but never rely on a rusty jacking point alone – use axle stands and chocks. Lever apart the A-frame bush to check it is intact. Wear here causes clonking on bumpy corners and the back of the car to move about. Sometimes a small stone can get lodged between the A-frame and the floor and make a mysterious rattle or tapping noise though usually it is the shock absorber bushes or valving that have

Sound, uncollapsed A-frame bush.

failed, or loose items in the boot or an exhaust tap. Check the wheel bearings for play or noise, or play in the universal joints, which act as both driveshaft and suspension links. Slight differential output

Check all visible brake pipes.

shaft float is acceptable, but reject anything over 1-2 millimetres, especially with leaking seal. V12s

Non-original dampers can snap.

and some supercharged models had a limited slip differential, which can be checked with both wheels off the ground, as they rotate the same way when one is turned with the transmission in neutral.

The handbrake cable should be oily and unfrayed. Handbrake shoes cannot be inspected without rear disc removal, which themselves should be largely corrosion free with no ridges.

It is difficult to check for play at the various inner rubber pivots and outer roller bearings, but a tyre lever and some judicious prying will reveal serious play. Good signs are pivot bolts dead centre in the bushes and fresh grease on all UJ nipples.

Front suspension, brakes & steering

Ex 4 Gd 3 Av 2 Po 1

X300/308s had a separate front subframe with rubber chassis vee mounts. This subframe can rust but most are okay – check by tapping and probing hard all over, as the scratches will not be seen and this is an important safety area, with replacement the only remedy. The long plush springs may hide a broken coil. Wishbone bushings can be visually inspected for perishing or swelling and play is easiest to check if the car is lowered onto spring pan supports so the suspension is in its normal orientation at mid-laden position. Dampers can be visually inspected for top or bottom mount break-up or

Top damper bushes perish.

fluid leakage and bounce each corner to check for damper condition. Look for tidy ABS and pad wear cables.

Check all ball joints for split gaiters and slack, and the anti-roll bar rubbers and drop links. Ask the seller to turn the steering while you feel for play at the track rod ends and look for rack movement in the bushings. This is serious because the rack bushes cannot be replaced, meaning a new rack is required. There are firm-up kits of nylon washers to fit either side of the mounts but these are tricky to install. Beware bodges with loops of wire and epoxy putty. Look for oil leaks from the power steering gear, although wet racks can just be under an engine leak. Look for the heat shields needed to stop exhaust heat damaging plastic or rubber rack parts.

Whilst under the car, especially if the undertray is missing, inspect the underside of the radiator support, the brake air ducts and sensors within them, the large bottom radiator hose and the radiator support bushings which are often missing or crumbled. Check the vented front discs for scoring and adequate pad thickness. Check for signs of cracked flex hoses or rusted brake pipes. The brake reservoir should have clean fluid without sediment.

Cabin trim

Ex 4   Gd 3   Av 2   Po 1

Even the oldest X300s can still look new inside, especially the rear seat and passenger side. A rough interior is a sign of neglect, though some seat bolster wear is almost inevitable as the miles accumulate. Seat frames also crack occasionally, which can be a problem to repair, plus position switches and potentiometers can go haywire. Musty smells mean water leaks, even if only from blocked air conditioner drains. Cubby box tops are vinyl on base models and can split or wear through. A cupholder is useful, but fragile if abused with large containers, so check it works. Consoles today often have holes where mobile phones were fitted. All cars used veneered dashboards though Sport models had plastic instrument surrounds. Headliners, by now, can be sagging slightly and are awkward to replace. Unless you have a special reason, only buy cars with full leather seats, as this is

Broken seat bracket repair.

what people expect in a Jaguar

Loose dash trim. Electrical gremlins?

Cracked frame causes driver's seat to lean.

when you come to sell. Only Daimler VDP models have totally leather cabin trim - lesser models using leather seat facings only. Check mirror and seat controls work and that under-dash trim is correctly secured.

Carpets

Ex 4   Gd 3   Av 2   Po 1

The carpets lie above moulded foam underlays. Sound-deadening anti-drum material is used extensively and can trap liquids. Check for holes, heavy wear or damp around the pedals, plus water from blocked AC drains in the centre, or from screen leaks at the sides. New carpets can hide terrible floors so lift to check. High-wear areas are vinyl faced but look for a car that has been used with floor mats so that the carpet is still good. Daimler/VDPs should have thick lambswool over-rugs.

Instruments and electrics

The first X300s had an analogue oil pressure gauge that can show variable pressure depending on conditions but all others had a 'fake' gauge, run off the oil pressure switch with a fixed resistance always showing mid scale. Check all gauges work but most importantly look for warning lights. See all of them illuminate before cranking the engine (to check none of the bulbs have been removed) and that they all go out once started. Cycle though the computer settings by pressing the left stalk, to see what historic fuel consumption has been (prepare for a surprise!). Try the OBD code scanner in the socket under the dash near the steering wheel and read off any codes (Chapter 7).

Non-veneered, but all dials work.

If you haven't already done so during road test, try every electrical function listed in the handbook. If fuse covers look recently disturbed, or there is insulating tape or a blown fuse in the ashtray be suspicious of electrical hassles. Look at the general condition of any visible wiring. There should be two remotes and they should open the boot when pressed twice quickly and should shut the windows and roof when pressed for several seconds.

Lights get grit-blasted dull.

The climate control is tested by switching the car off and holding 'Auto' and 'Recirc' buttons down while you restart it. Every panel display flashes and the system enters diagnostic mode. Press Auto again to see either a zero display or up to five stored error codes

Auto-dim mirrors can leak.

Radiator mounts perish over time.

(retrieved by cycling through using the Demist button). To clear any code press Demist and heated rear window buttons together. Code 23, low refrigerant pressure, is one of the most common, which prevents the compressor running. Next press Recirc to put the system in self-test mode, then press Face to cycle the system through all possible vent combinations, which gives noticeable changes of vent and fan operation.

The main ECU is very reliable but the CD ROM is needed to tell where the dozens of motors and computers are located. This is not needed at inspection time provided everything works electrically.

Cooling system

The X300/308 cooling systems are effective if kept clean and serviced. This includes removing debris between the AC condenser and the water radiator. The radiator mounts crumble, so check for a loose radiator. The water pump spindle should neither leak nor feel slack when pulled. The pump on an early V8 should be the later all-metal type, with the change noted in service records. The plastic thermostat housing on V8s can crack if mishandled and the large top hose can blow off. Some people fit worm-drive clips to prevent this.

Ex Gd Av Po
4 3 2 1

The plastic header tank should contain clean coolant at the correct level, with no bubbling or leaks along the seams. Look for fresh gaskets or hose clamps indicating recent replacement. The hose under the inlet manifold on sixes has notoriously poor access, leading to neglect that can destroy the engine if it blows at high speed. Hoses

Reliable 6-cylinder pump. V8 initially less so.

should be sound, with no corrosion around the alloy spigots. The top hose carries the hottest water and suffers first but if replaced others may then fail from age. X305s have fewer hoses than earlier V12s, but they are probably all coming up for replacement by now, which is a major task.

A cold fan clutch on V12s should stop spinning after about half a turn if the fan is flicked round. All other models use electric

Check fan clutch on V12.

fans so let the engine idle and check they cycle on and off correctly. Some X300s are wired to leave the fans on low speed permanently. Look at the long bolts in the thermostat housing on sixes, to see if there is heavy corrosion, as they have a habit of seizing or snapping when you need to change a thermostat.

Part of 'octopus hose.'

Fuel system

Ex Gd Av Po
4 3 2 1

A complete fuel injection system check requires specific test equipment but the OBD system will show many faults. Strange pulsing or a throbbing 'helicopter' type noise indicate a fuel pressure damper or hose problem. Injector connectors should be unbroken and firmly held by spring clips, with the wires not split or cracked where they emerge, or indeed anywhere else in the engine harness, which becomes brittle with age, especially on the V12 cars or on the cam cover of sixes. On sixes the breather hose from the cam cover can be full of oily deposits and the throttle body can require cleaning once a year on older engines depending on mileage. Early V8s were subject to a recall for a new throttle body to be fitted to prevent stalling at speed. Early X300s sometimes fail to register above ¾ tank full due to a sender problem.

Engine

The AJ16 engine is largely fault free and if the oil is clean and it blows no smoke and makes no odd noises it will probably run for years more. Supercharger bearing noise on the XJR is fairly obvious as is idler pulley screeching. Use a long probe or stethoscope if in doubt, but beware rotating components. Brief rattling on start up from cold is acceptable but Jaguar engines adjusted correctly should run with just a light rustle from the valve gear, once warm.

Old supercharger bearings rumble.

In checking if a V8 is a Nikasil engine, VIN numbers are not conclusive, since even after the first steel liner engine was fitted, others still received Nikasil motors from stock. A car made in late 2000 is probably not Nikasil, ditto most cars with five digit VIN numbers, but the only certain check is if your engine is numbered (effectively 'dated') after 0008181043, which refers to the first non-Nikasil engine made on 18th August 2000 at 10.43am. Failed engines replaced with steel-linered versions will

Listen for chain noise on V8s.

have a green ID tag on the crankcase behind the right cylinder head.

Some whirring from the timing chains is permissible but metallic clatter isn't. With clean oil and coolant and good service history a V8 should now last many years, although a Nikasil engine could theoretically fail any time. If the car has good history and is in other respects excellent then you may be happy to take the chance, but walk away from any rough Nikasil cars.

Traction control unit.

Transmission

Most X300/308s were ZF 4-speed automatics, with a Getrag 5-speed manual available outside North America. V12s and XJR used a GM truck gearbox for durability. All transmissions are generally reliable but not everlasting. It's therefore wise to keep money in reserve if buying a particularly high mileage example, or one with a tow bar. V8s with sealed transmissions that have never had an oil change are a risk and you should factor this into your price if the mileage is beyond about 80,000. Fluid level should only be checked when fully warmed up after a good run, and after moving through all the gear selector positions twice, to fill the valve block passages and avoid a falsely high reading. The V8 gearboxes are smoother but on all Jaguars the gear changes are largely imperceptible unless accelerating hard. Check the torque

Modest leak on AJ16 engine.

Transmission mount and shaft UJ.

converter lock-up operates around 50-52 mph, shown by a slight drop in revs at that speed on a light throttle. Dismiss any car with obvious drive problems such as noises or failure to move off immediately.

Manual gearboxes are refined and come with a very heavy leather-covered metal gear knob to smooth out changes. If fitted with a light wooden or plastic knob the gearchange quality can suffer. If there are noises when releasing the clutch, suspect a worn release bearing

Over-tightened split clutch resevoir cap.

or dry pilot bearing in the flywheel which may survive for years or break up suddenly. The small reservoir above the clutch pedal often has a snapped top due to ham-fisted over tightening. Clutch master cylinder rebuild kits are no longer available so budget for a complete assembly if the clutch feels soggy. The clutch and brake pedals each have return springs that can break, so check for lazy or sloppy actions.

Oil leaks

All X300/308 engines use proper garter type seals at the back of the crankshaft, so leakage from the bell housing is uncommon. Other leaks are usually fixable, so a very oily car has been neglected. The cam covers can leak both around the periphery and internally around the plug holes, which consequently fill with oil if the o-ring seals or covers are damaged. This eventually causes a misfire which shows up as an OBD code. One leak seen on some sixes is from a oil gallery in the head joint, near the distributor. It can leak badly, requiring head removal, but a faint weep can be left and monitored. V12s can leak from cam covers also, but the quality of gaskets used in these late engines is far better than classic Jaguars and leaks are comparatively infrequent. The V12s can also leak from the front seal and inspection plug or breather.

A cracked sump or stripped drain plug on any engine is bad news, although drips may just be from a hardened or missing copper washer.

The power steering reservoir is small and can be checked hot or cold on opposite sides of the dipstick. There should be no significant weeps anywhere in the steering system either from the pipework, pump or bellows on the rack, where rack seals wear out. Gearbox and differential will last a long time with oil drips, provided the levels are kept topped up.

Ignition

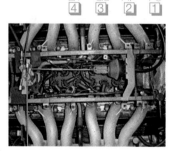

The ignition has no distributor on any X300/308, being completely computer controlled. The key part is the crank position sensor at the front of the engine (and another sensor at the back on some engines). This can get dirty and eventually fail but any such fault, like most others, will be shown as a code on the OBD system. Due to the generally fault-free, low-maintenance nature of the ignition, plugs can go long periods without being removed and can seize. It's a plus point if the service record shows plugs have been changed in the recent past or at least several times in the car's history.

Not even the V12 used a distributor.

Evaluation procedure

Add up the total points. Score: **96 = perfect; 72 = good; 48 = average; 24 = buyer beware!** Cars scoring over 67 should be completely useable and require the minimum of repair, although continued maintenance and care will be required to keep them in condition. Cars scoring between 24-48 will require serious restoration (at much the same cost regardless of score). Cars scoring between 50-68 will require very carefull assessment of necessary repair/restoration costs in order to reach a realistic value. Deduct four points from target total if a sunroof is not fitted.

There are still many X300/308s in daily use that feature in prestige car auctions but they are now tending to appear in down-market local auctions or specialist sales. If you are prepared to spend time looking round, these can be a fruitful source of good value cars, albeit probably not the cleanest or lowest mileage examples. For a good deal with some protection, or if you need to search for a specific model, auctions can be a good hunting ground.

Lined up for inspection.

Auction pros & cons

Pros: Prices will usually be lower than those of dealers and some private sellers, so you could pick up a real bargain. Auctioneers have usually established clear title with the seller, which is helpful and you can normally examine documentation relating to the vehicle and may get a 24hr of warranty.

Cons: You could drive far but lose the bidding. You may only get limited information beforehand and will not be able to test drive the car. Auction cars can also be scruffy. Check the level of buyer's premium payable on top of the hammer price – typically it's 5-7.5%.

For normal trade sales you just turn up on the day but for classic sales admission may be by advance catalogue, sometimes for two people, so take a friend. Even if you've tracked down your dream model and colour you need to decide a price limit and stick to it, with your friend reminding you to stop, if necessary! Being caught up in 'auction fever' can mean paying too much and because the buyer's premium increases pro-rata, you are hit twice and any problems with the car will seem all the more annoying.

Payment details

All auction firms publish terms and conditions, describing charges and acceptable payment methods. For trade sales the cars go through and make whatever they make, but for catalogue sales there are normally price estimates. Full or immediate part-payment or a deposit are usually requested, with the balance payable within 24 hours. Look at the small print for cash and credit card limits and options such as personal cheques, debit cards or bank drafts. The car won't be released until paid for, with storage at your cost until completion.

Follow the traders.

Preview day

Typical weekly trade auctions are freewheeling events with content lists often viewable on-line in advance. Few X300/306s will be in specialist classic auctions with preview days. Auction staff or sellers may start the cars and will normally drive them through the auction. You are permitted to look underneath but not jack the car up yourself. Take a torch and possibly a mirror on a stick for a better view.

Auction day

Cars are sold in order of lot number so get there earlier for low number lots. Phrases such as 'It's with me at ...' mean the car hasn't yet reached reserve. 'It's for sale at ...' means the car has reached reserve and will now sell to the highest bidder. Cars still unsold when the hammer drops may be open to offers via the auctioneer.

eBay & the internet

eBay & other online auctions cover the best and the worst of the auction spectrum. If you are bidding very low and do not mind the resultant car being poor because you have risked so little, then you can get a great deal. The author himself has bought several cheap Jaguars sight unseen and not been disappointed. Tread warily, however, because by now there are enough poor X300/308s being auctioned that you are no longer as likely to get a sound car.

Most on-line sources show the seller's location, and may even allow you to search by distance from home, which can be useful. Always check, however, that the car is actually at the seller's location. Opinion is divided on whether it is better to choose your upper limit and bid that at the outset, or let yourself be possibly carried away as the auction nears its end by bidding and re-bidding in the dying moments.

Remember, too, that it will be very difficult to obtain satisfaction if a dishonest seller disappears with your money, or a car never arrives because it never existed. On-line payment schemes provide some protection, as does use of a credit card, but the onus will still be on you to do all the running and work hard to recover any losses.

Auctioneers

Barrett-Jackson www.barrett-jackson.com/ Bonhams www.bonhams.com/ British Car Auctions BCA) www.bca-europe.com or www.british-car-auctions.co.uk/ Cheffins www.cheffins.co.uk/ Christies www.christies.com/ Coys www.coys.co.uk/ eBay www.ebay.com/ H&H www.classic-auctions.co.uk/ RM www.rmauctions.com/ hannons www.shannons.com.au/ Silver www.silverauctions.com

11 Paperwork
– correct documentation is essential!

Follow the paper trail

These cars are modern and, until recently, expensive. Most were sold to wealthy people or companies. Therefore, a complete dealer service record should be present, and lack of records is a serious demerit. There should still be a full set of factory handbooks and radio security codes, etc. Cheap cars with no service history or other paperwork are doubtful prospects, unless you judge their condition or value to be excellent using this book. When you come to sell, the lack of papers will hurt your sale too. Supplying dealers are probably still in existence, and the service location may remember the car and be able to give insight to any major items, such as engine or gearbox replacement on V8s.

The more history the better.

Low mileage cars are not necessarily better and in some cases can be worse if regular servicing based on time as well as distance was not carried out. Be especially careful with low-mileage '97-2000 V8s which may have been used for short trips and may be about to expire from Nikasil wear, even though the chances of surviving are better now that low-sulphur petrol is used everywhere.

Paperwork must match the car VIN.

For the V12s especially, good documentation is almost essential.

Although the X300/308 is not yet an historic car, rarer models such as the V12 or other immaculate examples should see values climb in the medium term. A good history file would help value so items like the original bill of sale, handbook, parts invoices and repair or parts bills all add to the story of the car. A correct brochure for the car's model year, or original contemporary road test, is useful.

Registration documents

Beware a private seller who has only just acquired the car they are selling. Why are they selling on so quickly? Lack of ownership certification normally means extra care is needed with the seller. Where documents do exist, check that serial numbers actually match the car. Sellers should issue a signed, dated and addressed receipt.

Roadworthiness certificate

Even the newest X308 is now over five years old, and most markets require regular roadworthiness checks every year or two. Tests are usually carried out at approved locations and a sheaf of old certificates is useful to confirm the car's mileage and history, since odometers can be altered.

Certificates of authenticity

Because these cars are recent, there is little interest in historical provenance. However, if you would like to pursue your car's history from day one, the Jaguar Daimler Heritage Trust (www.jdht.com) provides Production Record Trace Certificates for a small fee to those who can prove ownership and supply copies of the car VIN and title document. The certificate confirms build and dispatch dates, specification and trim codes, model type, original colours, original selling distributor and sometimes the first owner and registration number.

Manuals needed for a complex car.

Valuation certificate

The vast majority of X300/308 cars will be valued by market price guides like most other cars. If you have an especially rare model or historically significant car such as a pre-production prototype then a valuation certificate may be appropriate to secure 'agreed value' insurance that would pay out above the value of a normal car of the same age and specification. They are most unlikely to be offered by a seller and should be ignored in any case; base the value on your own assessment using this book.

www.velocebooks.com / www.veloce.co.uk
All current books • New book news • Special offers • Gift vouchers

12 What's it worth to you?
– let your head rule your heart!

Condition

If the car passes inspection you should offer a figure based on the sale price, adjusted by your findings (Chapter 9). Allow for repairing any faults, and use values in the classic car press or current price guides to support your offer.

'Pimped' cars lose value.

Give your offer credibility by providing auction values reported in the press, or eBay prices, which are extremely low for many cars. Some X300/308 owners may not realise how much their car has depreciated in even a short time, and will need persuading of the very low value of what is usually still a fine car. However, with the price of fuel rising, others will be glad to sell their car at almost any price, needing the space and money for something more economical. For a non-standard car you'll have to decide which deviations from standard enhance value and which detract from it.

Desirable options/extras

There are few aftermarket customisation options for these cars, so radical revisions are very rare. Most are still original except for one or two accessories such as a cup holder armrest or half-wood steering wheel which enhance the car's value. Some owners have put later X308 bumpers, wheels and lights on earlier X300 models and, although this certainly makes them look more up-to-date from the outside, buyers may prefer a standard car. Upgrades such as full electric seats on a base model, or reversing sensors or headlamp washers increase value. The more high-spec

Neat Jag accessory stone guards.

the car originally, the less likely it is that anything much can be done to it to boost saleability. In-car entertainment upgrades, or special paint and wheels, are options, but there are few cars are so equipped.

Unlike the XJ40 self-levelling suspension, which was sometimes unreliable and expensive to fix, the CATS damping system is a good upgrade and, although very hard to retro-fit, does add value if present. Wheels from the later X350 XJ cars do

45

not fit, but those from the 1996-on XK8/XKR range do. These look suitably sporty whilst still being identifiably 'Jaguar', but do check the wheels don't rub on full lock or full bump. A clear upgrade is to fit any Jaguar production alloy wheel to a base model originally sold with steel wheels, as many XJ6 cars were in Europe, particularly 3.2 models. Likewise, substituting full leather seating for part-leather, or retro-fitting extras such as cruise control or air conditioning from a higher spec model onto an entry level car, helps value. However, it is generally best to ignore base-level models anyway, since they offer only basic equipment and are harder to resell. You should concentrate on fully-equipped cars, unless you have a very specific reason to do otherwise, such as searching out a manual car (which were often entry-level models).

Standard exhausts were low-grade stainless but need replacing after about ten years, when better 304 grade aftermarket stainless can be fitted. Mid-catalyst substitute pipes help exhaust note, economy and power (VERY slightly), as do silencer substitute pipes, but may be technically illegal in some jurisdictions. A good car should pass inspection with functional Lambda feedback operation and only primary down-pipe catalysts. AJ6 Engineering provides dyno-proven extractor systems for 6s and V12s.

Too much is too much.

There are no electronic ignition or engine management upgrades available or needed, and if an owner has 'chipped' a car it might well spell trouble at servicing or repair time. Sport dampers are green and touring dampers are black. Sports dampers can usefully firm up a soggy touring suspension and might be considered desirable, as might fitting a rear anti-roll bar to a model not originally using one.

A manual transmission conversion is not everyone's choice for a luxury car but generally is worth having if fuel economy and performance are higher on your list than convenience or purchase price.

Chrome – liked by some.

There is only one source of manual transmissions for V8 models but several vendors sell kits for the sixes or even the V12. Sometimes the entire transmission can be fitted from a manual donor car, including pedal box, console items and gearbox mount. The conversion is very easy for 3.2 cars which did not use an electronic automatic box but some fiddling may be required to emulate the transmission ECU's signals to the main car systems on 4.0L and 6.0L models. The V12 does not have the same bell housing bolt pattern as earlier 5.3L cars, for which more manuals are available, but the 6.0L block can be drilled to suit as the bosses are still present.

Liquefied gas fuel conversions are desirable in markets where a suitable filling point infrastructure exists. Even XJR cars can run on gas, but the costs of installation are high and are not recovered early unless high mileages are driven.

Undesirable features

Cloth trim is usually a turn-off, although it can be comfortable in extremes of heat and cold. The early 3.2 base models with no air-conditioning are poor value and be sure to check a seller is not using 'climate control' (which all X300 cars have) to cover for missing refrigeration on these models (N.B. all V8s have air conditioning).

A few cars have been heavily modified ('pimped') and these will probably be very hard to sell except to the rare buyers who value outrageous customising just because it is different, or offers hundreds of watts of sound power.

Converted former automatics can sometimes take longer to sell because more people expect a Jaguar to be automatic, but the increased economy offered by a carefully-driven manual may gradually change that as fuel prices move relentlessly upward.

Impractical but iconic trays.

Screen leaks and dropped headlinings can make a car almost unsaleable if better examples are available locally. Dull or non-metallic colours generally sell slower than metallic colours. A tow bar can spell a hard-worked transmission and often puts off buyers, as can poorly-fitted or non-Jaguar body kits, or excessively large or showy wheels.

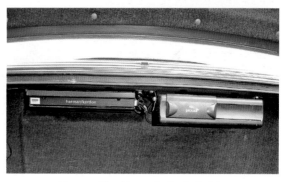

Harman Kardon audio is desirable.

13 Do you really want to restore?

– it'll take longer and cost more than you think

X300/308 cars are not old enough to require wholesale restoration in the ususal sense of the word. They are also sufficiently plentiful that there is no need to buy a poor car to save money, since good cars are not too expensive.

Therefore there is no classic 'restoration' to be done, but the equivalent would be refurbishing or recommissioning a car which has either been stolen, damaged or left off the road for a period. As always, it is normally easier, cheaper and quicker to search out a good example than to try and rectify significant faults on a poor car. Having said that, if there is a specific car, such as a manual XJR or an otherwise excellent V8 that has been sidelined with cam chain or Nikasil trouble, it can make some kind of sense to put the car back into action rather than break it for spare parts. Such a car should come very cheap, to account for the money that will need to be spent.

Can you repair air conditioning?

Setting out to repair a car that is already in need of major work is certainly not cost-effective and unlikely to be especially satisfying either, unless you obtain the car for very little, or mainly want to learn your way around Jaguars. New body shells are available but there is a huge amount of work involved in re-shelling a car which is much more focused on today's complex wiring circuitry than it is with old classics and simple technology.

Repairing or even diagnosing faults in an X300/308 is nothing like repairing

Damage is more than skin deep.

a simple older car, as there are lots of electronic components and circuits which can't be checked – much less repaired – without specialist knowledge and some equipment. This puts them in a different class to simpler cars from an earlier era, which are never likely to disappoint an owner due to spiralling costs or complexity of repair. If you have never restored a car before, you should start with a simple, smaller model.

Even if you already have a poor car, or have decided to buy one in need of work, ask yourself whether it makes sense. The author purchased possibly the most corroded X300 in the UK, but this was justified, because it is not only a very early car but a very rare manual XJR model, and likely to provide unmatched fun in the long term. For your dream V12 or Daimler Super V8 you may consider doing something similar, but do not underestimate the task or attempt it with only basic tools and facilities.

The interiors of these cars wear very well and apart from the driver's seat it should be possible to buy even the very earliest car that still looks like new inside, or very close. Therefore if a car is actually bad inside it is likely the mechanical parts have been similarly neglected and the car is probably going to be a huge headache.

Whilst the 6-cylinder engines are not too hard to work on, the big V12 is bulky and complex and can swallow a lot of specialist hours to refurbish properly. Thankfully, most are still in good condition but this is by no means assured after a minimum 12 years of possibly variable maintenance. The V8s can be worked on but are delicate and complex. Treat with caution!

Think about the type of work you are realistically capable of, then calculate the likely budget for a professional doing the other repairs. Then double it since you are likely to overspend heavily. Some people love engines or electrics but can't do structural body work or paint. Be realistic and recognize that it's easy to over-commit, especially if you've a definite schedule in mind for the car to be ready. Good specialist workshops are usually booked up in advance and are not cheap.

Budget for some special tools for both the chassis and power train. For example, the big V12 weighs around 700lb, which is more than many normal engine stands can safely manage.

There are more and more cars being broken for spares as an alternative to paying dealer's prices for original parts or generic prices for possibly questionable Far Eastern aftermarket items. The cars are not so rare that the whole project cannot be abandoned and a better car sought, with the original serving as a donor for spares or sold off piecemeal.

Don't even think about a re-shell.

Cloth sells less well.

Minor rust repairs can be awkward to do properly.

www.velocebooks.com / www.veloce.co.uk
All current books • New book news • Special offers • Gift vouchers

14 Paint problems

– a bad complexion, including dimples, pimples and bubbles

X300/308 cars have curvaceous bodywork with light lines supplemented by swooping swages and trim highlights. They are supremely handsome but do require good paint to show well. Even some factory finish can be dimpled in a few areas but generally the paint was done to a high standard and mirror polished. Paint flaws can detract markedly from the overall appeal of a car, even if the structure is sound underneath. Some of the most vulnerable panels are detachable and accessible from both sides so it ought to be simple enough to ensure a good paint job, but in many cases corners are cut and the car exits the paint shop with superficially good paint that later gives trouble in one of the classic ways described below.

Clouding/peeling

This is probably the single most common paint problem on unmolested cars. Otherwise good large panels, such as bonnet, roof or boot lid, can be spoiled by patches of lifted clear coat lacquer. It is normally due to UV damage and as well as a bare dull central area there is a halo of lighter peeling lifted lacquer. Repair is not simple, since merely re-applying clear coat over base will not adequately match the faded paint colour. Poorly applied re-spray paint may also peel, especially near the tops of doors or around windows where preparation was inadequate next to masked-off areas. Repair is a specialist job and may well require a topcoat strip and entire panel repaint to avoid a 'patched' appearance.

Non-original undertray paint lifting.

Classic lacquer peel.

Orange peel

This is as an uneven paint surface looking like a dimpled orange skin, caused by atomized paint droplets not flowing into each other on the painted surface. Common areas are the vertical panels such as rear boot area or front of bonnet and headlight surrounds. It's sometimes possible to polish out with paint cutting compound or very fine abrasive paper on a soft block. A re-spray is necessary in severe cases so consult a bodywork repairer/paint shop for advice. If the paint is two-pack, it will be very hard to flatten. Note that due to production tolerances some X300/308s will not have glass-smooth paint from the factory. This also applies to other modern cars, so the point at which orange peel is classed as a 'problem' is partly subjective.

Slight orange peel from new.

Cracking and crazing

Few X300s, let alone X308s, should have gross paint problems, though modest past repairs may not have been done in compatible systems. As well as such mismatches, over time some original paints have suffered in extreme climates, and for non-original paint all bets are off. Severe cracking is often caused by too heavy an application of paint (or filler beneath). For two-pack modern finishes, insufficient stirring of the paint before application can lead to the components being improperly mixed, resulting in cracking. Incompatibility with the paint already on the panel can have a similar effect by crazing. Factory paints can craze in desert climates or sometimes even in milder environments, and is usually worst on horizontal panels. Rectification requires stripping entirely or rubbing down to a sound finish before re-spraying.

Deep scratches beyond topcoat.

Blistering

This is typically caused by corrosion of the metal beneath the paint. Found on the wheelarches or sill seams, the damage can be superficial or signify deeper problems. The metal will have to be repaired before repainting. Micro-blistering is usually caused when moisture penetrates the primer before top coat spraying. Consult a paint specialist, though damaged paint will usually have to be removed before partial or full re-spray. Also caused by car covers that don't 'breathe' and encourage moisture absorption.

Bad blistering over untreated metal.

Fading

Some colours, especially reds, fade under strong sunlight, even with polish protection. Sometimes paint restorers or cutting compounds can restore colour; but a re-spray may be the only solution if you're unhappy driving a car with serious 'patina.'

Dimples

Dimples or craters in the paintwork are caused by residues of polish (particularly silicone) not being removed properly before re-spraying. Paint removal and repainting is the only solution – localized if possible, extensive if necessary. Remember: this problem was caused by insufficient care in the first place ...

Dents

Small dents are usually easily remedied by a 'Dentmaster,' or equivalent technician, who can pull or push out the dent (if the paint surface is still intact). Companies offering dent removal services usually come to your home: consult your telephone directory or ask at a local prestige car dealer for personal recommendation.

Being a large, moderately thirsty car and bordering on classic status, X300/308 Jaguars are prime candidates for 'part-time' use. This is understandable, but a pity. Like most cars they work best when worked often. Even if the 20-30,000-mile years are behind them, it is still wise to use them frequently. If for any reason you buy a car that has been stood for a while, the key points to note are set out on the following pages.

A drive of at least ten miles, once a week, is helpful for the X300 but is barely adequate for the X305 V12 and the V8s. These both have fast warm-up technology but nevertheless respond best to being thoroughly warm for a good period. Try for longer runs and avoid frequently starting the engine and switching off before totally hot, such as when merely moving it around. Apart from an over-fuelling glitch that can flood the car, it encourages build up of condensation, which is bad for the internals. Whitish deposits on the oil filler cap or dipstick are a tell-tale sign.

Depending on storage conditions, the interior leather can also benefit from feeding while out of use. Driving also helps disperse plasticizers in the tyre carcass to keep it supple.

Lay-up hurts Jags.

Seized or sluggish components

The X300/308s have single-piston sliding calipers front and rear, which can become sticky on their pins and bind. Pistons can seize too, shown by dragging or slow-to-release brakes. The best way to maintain brakes is to use them and change the fluid prior to extended lay-up. The ABS valve block uses a large multi-pin connector which can deteriorate and light the ABS dashboard warning lamp after being stood for a few weeks outside. Dirt on the wheel sensors can do the same and the left rear wheel sensor also feeds data to the traction control system whose warning might also illuminate. A dirty crank position sensor can also throw a code. The handbrake shoes can bind inside the hubs if left on in humid conditions.

For manual transmission cars the clutch friction plate may seize to the pressure plate or flywheel from corrosion, so regularly working through the gears and easing the clutch to and fro whilst the engine warms up helps, if it is not practicable to exercise the car because of heavy snow for example.

Fluids

Old, acidic, engine oil will corrode bearings and machined surfaces, as will 'fresh' oil repeatedly loaded with products of combustion from briefly starting up a large cold engine. Automatics benefit from a change to fresh fluid with fresh corrosion inhibitors before a long lay-up, though this is not normally practical.

Out of date antifreeze or plain water will spoil alloy water passages over time so be sure it is up to specification before storing. Brake fluid absorbs water from the atmosphere and should be renewed every 2-3 years. If renewing pads, push back the pistons after opening the bleed valve so old contaminated fluid does not get pushed back into the pipework. Power steering fluid is normally OK to leave, within reason. The large hidden washer fluid bottle can grow algae and block pipes if plain water is left for months.

Use fuel stabilizer additives, although opinions differ on whether it is better to fill to the brim to minimize condensation inside the tank, or to almost run the fuel down and stabilize the remainder, prior to adding fresh fuel at the earliest opportunity on recommissioning, to dilute any stale fuel.

Tyres

X300/308s are often fitted with Pirellis, which have a reputation for flat-spotting quickly. Tyre walls may crack or bulge and have an approximately 6-8 year shelf life depending on conditions. Regular use helps preserve tyres by dispersing the plasticizers throughout the compound. Avoid high temperatures and strong sunlight and replace poor tyres if in doubt. Storing on blocks is kind to tyres but hard work.

Shock absorbers (dampers)

With lack of use, the dampers can corrode on the piston rod. There are no special problems with the CATS system, if fitted.

Rubber and plastic

Radiator hoses can perish and split, possibly resulting in loss of all coolant – leading to rapid death in the case of the V8 motor especially. The large hose from the pump to the block (under the inlet manifold) is often neglected and deterioration can continue in storage. There are very many hoses for oil, fuel, water, vacuum and brake fluid that can deteriorate from heat or ozone or solvents - or just harden with age. Wiper blades will also harden eventually, especially at high ambient temperatures or outside in strong UV.

Electrics
The security system exerts a small current drain as does the clock. Preserving the battery over long periods requires a trickle charger and ideally the battery removed (to prevent corrosive vapours condensing on the boot metalwork). Earthing/grounding problems are common when the connections have corroded. Modern sealed multi-plugs electrical connectors abound on the X300/308, but damp can still affect them and dielectric grease is useful here.

Exhaust
Exhaust fumes contain water and acids, so even the ferritic stainless factory exhausts eventually corrode. This can also be from the inside when the car is not used, or is shut off before totally warmed up. The X300/308 has twin exhausts and the surface area is quite large so condensation is an issue if the system is not high-grade stainless. Rubber hangers deteriorate and can come off.

LPG systems can deteriorate if not used.

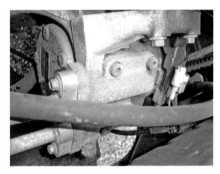
Unused AC compressors leak.

16 The Community

– key people, organisations and companies in the XJ world

The X300/308 has been many people's first Jaguar, having gained a reputation for reliability and user-friendliness. They are also so inexpensive that they're practical as an occasional 'fun' car and as a large safe car for wives and children to drive on crowded roads - insurance permitting.

Plenty of X300/308s are still daily drivers for people to whom they are just a roomy vehicle. Yet because they exude elegance and refinement they have seduced lots of enthusiasts and X300/308s are very common Jaguars amongst club members – including those with a classic Jag in their garage. Dealers are still happy to service and supply spares and many independents are equipping themselves with the electronic gadgetry needed to programme key transponders, ECUs, diagnose complex problems etc. Many cars are also in breaker's yards as a source of second-hand parts.

There is a dedicated forum to all Series X300/308 models on the internet at www.jag-lovers.org and dedicated sections in the key Jaguar magazines such as Jaguar World Monthly and most major club publications.

Clubs

Jaguar Drivers' Club
18 Stuart Street, Luton, Bedfordshire LU1 2SL
Tel: +44 (0)1582 419332
www.jaguardriver.co.uk
Set up with factory support originally and covering the full range of Jaguars. Has a good web site, excellent magazine and much X300/308 support, insurance schemes and offers valuations etc. Extensive overseas network.

Jaguar Enthusiasts' Club
Abbeywood Office Park, Emma Chris Way
Filton, Bristol BS34 7JU
Tel: +44 (0)1179 698186
www.jec.org.uk
World's largest Jaguar club, offering the usual good magazine as well as tool hire, specially-commissioned spares and events for every taste. Also very useful JagAds internet and print-based advertisement facility.

Jaguar Clubs of North America
c/o Nelson Rath, 1000 Glenbrook, Anchorage, KY 40223
Tel: +1 502 244 1672
www.jcna.com
Good web site, technical articles and US club network and events calendar. An umbrella organisation for the network of local and regional clubs in the USA.

The Jaguar Daimler Heritage Trust
Browns Lane, Allesley, Coventry, CV5 9DR
Tel: +44 (0)2476 202141
www.jdht.com

Holders of the official Jaguar archives on production numbers, build configuration and dispatch details, sometimes including first owner information. Sponsored by the Jaguar company in the USA and UK to supply manuals etc and Heritage Certificates confirming the originality of your car's major components. The CD ROM Manuals are not perfect but the only thing widely available.

Parts suppliers

SNG Barratt Group Ltd
UK, USA, Holland, France and Germany addresses
See www.sngbarratt.com
Biggest and best? One of the oldest and most comprehensive spares sources for Jaguars. Bases in USA/UK/Europe including full modern Jaguar spares operation, not merely classics.

David Manners
991 Oldbury Road, Oldbury,
West Midlands B69 4RJ, UK
Tel 0121 544 4040
www.davidmanners.co.uk
Wide range of modern parts for Jaguar and Daimler.

XKs Unlimited
850 Fiero Lane
San Luis Obispo, CA 93401, USA
Tel 805 544 7864
www.xks.com
Good West Coast supplier with clear line drawings in catalogue and website ordering system.

Coventry West Inc
2101 Randall Rd
Lithonia, GA 30058, USA
Tel 1 800 331 2193
www.coventrywest.com
Possibly the best North American source for new, refurbished or used modern Jaguar parts. Very friendly and helpful. Offer rebuilding service for differentials, etc.

Useful sources

The best source of detailed information – though there are gaps – are the CD ROM manuals (one each for X300/305/308) produced from official Jaguar manuals by the JDHT. See their web site above.

Another electronic option would be a subscription to AllData (www.alldata.com).

Jag-Lovers
www.jag-lovers.org
This is an excellent web-only resource, with great on-line books including the X300 and discussion forums for X300/308s in all versions. Join now and donate a percentage of what it saves you – worth every penny.

Jaguar World Monthly

An excellent independent monthly magazine by Kelsey Publishing (www.jaguar-world.com). Has regular news and features on the X300/308. Many trade advertisements and includes American pages with adverts relevant to the USA.

The on-line X300 Book

Author: Various contributors. Available as a free download at http://www.jag-lovers.org/ebooks/bookindex.php?Vbook=x300 and extremely useful for most systems. Best downloaded complete and then printed in sections as and when required.

The XJ-S Book

Author: Kirbert Palm and contributors. Another free download from Jag-Lovers and regarded by many as the definitive collection of all things V12, at least in terms of the engine itself. Written for the XJ-S rather than the X305, but useful for learning about V12 engine despite little specific X305 information.

Jaguar XJ-S, The Essential Buyers Guide

Author: Peter Crespin. A practical and highly-illustrated hands-on guide, to take you step-by-step through examination and purchase of Jaguar's longest-running production car of all – the legendary XJ-S Grand Tourer. Covering all engine and body configurations, this book shows what to look for, what to avoid, and whether the car is likely to suit your needs, plus relative values and the best places to buy.

Jaguar XJ-S

Author: Brian Long. The definitive history of Jaguar's E-Type replacement, the XJ-S. More a grand tourer than a sportscar, the controversially styled XJ-S offered a combination of supercar performance and grand tourer luxury. Includes rare photos of the prototypes that didn't make production.

Haynes manuals:

There are no Haynes manuals for any of the cars covered in this book. The closest, which covers similar suspension, fuelling and body systems for the normally-aspirated models is the XJ40 manual:

Jaguar XJ6 & Sovereign Oct 86-Sept 94 & Service and Repair Manual (#3621)

ISBN 1859602614
Author: Mike Stubblefield
Hardback: c.200pp

Jaguar & Daimler 12-cylinder Owners Workshop Manual

ISBN 1850102775
Author: Peter G Strasman
Hardback: 410pp
Good practical guide, not really for the XJ305 but many similarities with the 6.0L engine used.

17 Vital statistics
– essential data at your fingertips

X300/X305 production (Jaguar, Daimler/VDP combined)

Normally aspirated	Supercharged	6.0 V12	Total*
81,326	6547	4165	92,038

*Around 2% of 6-cylinder cars were manuals.

X308 production 97-2002 (Jaguar, Daimler/VDP combined)

Normally aspirated	Supercharged	Total
107,726	18,534	126,260

The above numbers are provided with grateful thanks to Anders Ditlev Clausager, Chief Archivist at the Jaguar Daimler Heritage Trust in Coventry.

Technical specifications by model
Specifications changed between years, models and markets, so only an indicative summary is possible here. Please check the appropriate information for specific models/years and markets from other sources, such as original brochures found at www.jag-lovers.org

X300 – produced 1994.5-1997.5
3.2: Inline 6-cylinder 24V DOHC, 3239 cm^3, 91 x 83mm, 216bhp @ 5100rpm & 232lb/ft @ 4500rpm
4.0: Inline 6-cylinder 24V DOHC, 3980cm^3, 91 x 102mm, 245bhp @ 4800rpm & 289lb/ft @ 4000rpm (XJR:322bhp @ 5000rpm & 378lb/ft @ 3050rpm)
6.0: ('94.5-96) V12 cylinder SOHC, 5993cm^3, 90 x 78.5mm, 313bhp @ 5350rpm & 353lb/ft @ 2850rpm

X308 – produced 1997.5-2003.5
3.2: V8 cylinder 32V DOHC, 3248cm^3, 86 x 70mm, 240bhp @ 6350rpm & 233lb/ft @ 4350rpm
4.0: V8 cylinder 32V DOHC, 3996cm^3, 86 x 86mm, 290bhp @ 6100rpm & 290lb/ft @ 4250rpm (XJR: 370bhp @ 6150rpm & 387lb/ft @ 3600rpm)

All models
Transmission
Manual 6-cyl: Getrag 290 5-speed overdrive gearbox. Twin-mass flywheel.
Automatic 6-cyl: ZF 4-speed, with electronic mode selection on 4.0L models.
Automatic 6-cyl Supercharged and V12: GM 4L80E 4-speed electronic mode selection. on 4.0L models
Automatic V8: Electronic 5-speed with electronic mode selection.

Length: 16ft 5.8in (5024mm). width (inc. mirrors): 6ft 9.7in (2074mm).
Height: 4ft 3.7in (1314mm)
Weight: 3968-4354lb/1800-1974kg depending on model.

Suspension: Fully independent unequal length wishbone at the front, incorporating anti-dive geometry and mounted on a rubber-isolated subframe with anti-roll bar. Independent rear suspension, with a lower wishbone and upper driveshaft link, using a single coil spring/damper unit per side. CATS adaptive damping on some models.

Brakes: ABS ventilated power-assisted outboard disc brakes at each corner, with ABS on almost all models.

Steering: Variable power-assisted, with tilt/telescopic column. 16in wheels on most models with 17in on supercharged X300 and some V8 designs. 18in on V8 supercharged models.

The Essential Buyer's Guide™

The Essential Buyer's Guide
ALFA ROMEO GIULIA
GT COUPE

978-1-904788-69-0

The Essential Buyer's Guide
ALFA ROMEO GIULIA
SPIDER

978-1-904788-98-0

The Essential Buyer's Guide
BMW
GS

978-1-84584-135-5

The Essential Buyer's Guide
BSA
Bantam
All models 1948 to 1971

978-1-84584-165-2

The Essential Buyer's Guide
BSA
500 & 650 Twins
A7, A10, A50 & A65 1946 to 1973

978-1-84584-136-2

The Essential Buyer's Guide
CITROEN
2CV

978-1-845840-99-0

The Essential Buyer's Guide
CITROEN
DS & ID
All models
1966 to 1975

978-1-84584-138-6

The Essential Buyer's Guide
FIAT
500 & 600 1955 to 1992
Saloons/Sedans, Multipla, Giardiniera & 126

978-1-84584-147-8

The Essential Buyer's Guide
JAGUAR
E-type
3.8 & 4.2 litre

978-1-904788-85-0

The Essential Buyer's Guide
JAGUAR
E-type
V12 5.3 litre

978-1845840-77-8

The Essential Buyer's Guide
Jaguar/Daimler
XJ

978-1-84584-200-0

The Essential Buyer's Guide
JAGUAR
XJ-S
All 6- and 12-cylinder models
1975 to 1996

978-1-84584-161-4

The Essential Buyer's Guide
JAGUAR/DAIMLER
XJ6, XJ12 & Sovereign
All Jaguar/Daimler XJ6 series I, II & III
models 1968 to 1992

978-1-845841-19-5

The Essential Buyer's Guide
Triumph
TR6

978-1-845840-26-6

The Essential Buyer's Guide
MERCEDES-BENZ PAGODA
230, 250 & 280SL
W113 series Roadsters & Coupés
1963 to 1971

978-1-845841-13-3

The Essential Buyer's Guide
MERCEDES-BENZ
280-560SL & SLC
W107 series Roadsters & Coupés
1971 to 1989

978-1-845841-07-2

The Essential Buyer's Guide
MG
MGB MGB GT

978-1-845840-29-7

The Essential Buyer's Guide
MORRIS
MINOR & 1000
Saloons, Travellers & Convertibles
1952 to 1971

978-1-845841-01-0

The Essential Buyer's Guide
PORSCHE
928

978-1-904788-70-6

The Essential Buyer's Guide
ROLLS-ROYCE
SILVER SHADOW
BENTLEY
T-SERIES
including Corniche, Camargue, Silver
Shadow II & Bentley T2: 1965 to 1995

978-1-84584-146-1

The Essential Buyer's Guide
SUBARU
Impreza
All turbo models 1994 to 2007

978-1-84584-163-8

The Essential Buyer's Guide
TRIUMPH
BONNEVILLE

978-1-84584-134-8

The Essential Buyer's Guide
MINI

978-1-84584-204-8

The Essential Buyer's Guide
VOLKSWAGEN
BEETLE

978-1-904788-72-0

The Essential Buyer's Guide
VOLKSWAGEN
BUS

978-1-845840-22-8

The Essential Buyer's Guide
Volkswagen
GOLF GTI

978-1-84584-188-1

The Essential Buyer's Guide
Jaguar/Daimler
XJ40

978-1-84584-192-8

£9.99*/$19.95*

*prices subject to change • p&p extra • for more details visit www.veloce.co.uk or email info@veloce.co.uk

Also from Veloce Publishing:

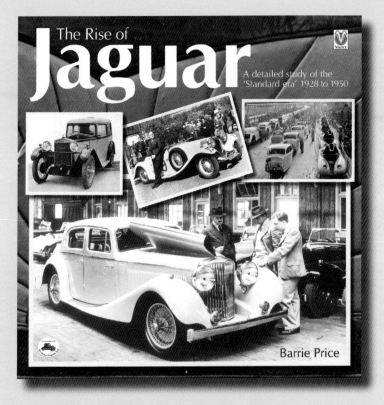

Hardback • £37.50* • 176 pages • 265 photos
• ISBN: 978-1-904788-27-0

A study of how SS metamorphosed into Jaguar, how the company prospered &
grew (even during the world's worst economic depression) and the importance
of the relationship with the Standard Motor Company. Many hitherto unknown
facts disclosed. Copiously illustrated with superb & evocative contemporary

*p&p extra. Call 01305 260068 for details. Prices subject to change.

www.velocebooks.com / www.veloce.co.uk
All current books • New book news • Special offers • Gift vouchers

Also from Veloce Publishing:

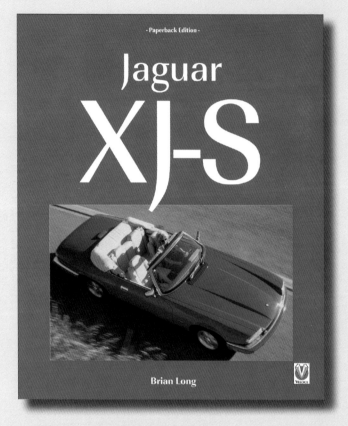

- Paperback Edition -

Jaguar
XJ-S

Brian Long

**Paperback • 19.99* • 192 pages • 254 colour & b&w photos
• ISBN: 978-1-904788-20-1**

The definitive history of Jaguar's E-Type replacement, the XJ-S. More a grand tourer
than a sportscar, the controversially styled XJ-S offered a combination of supercar
performance and grand tourer luxury. Includes rare photos of the prototypes that
didn't make production.

*p&p extra. Call 01305 260068 for details. Prices subject to change.

www.velocebooks.com / www.veloce.co.uk
All current books • New book news • Special offers • Gift vouchers

Also from Veloce Publishing:

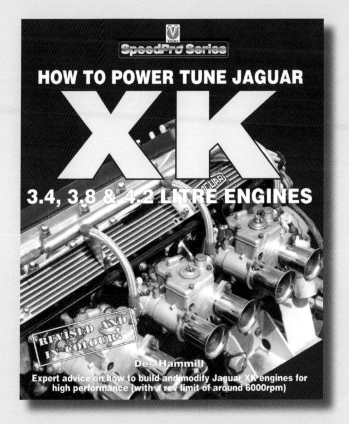

Paperback • £19.99* • 128 pages • 51 colour pictures • ISBN: 978-1-84584-005-1

Full details on camshafts, camshaft timing, valve springs and cylinder head options and modifications. Carburation chapters cover: 1¾ and 2 inch twin SU setups; triple 2 inch SUs; and triple Weber and Dellorto setups. A special section is included on modifying SUs for improved engine performance, along with the relevant needle specifications. Full details on ignition systems and timing, exhaust manifolds and systems and general tune-up information.

*p&p extra. Call 01305 260068 for details. Prices subject to change.

www.velocebooks.com / www.veloce.co.uk
All current books • New book news • Special offers • Gift vouchers

Index

www.velocebooks.com / www.veloce.co.uk

All current books • New book news • Special offers • Gift vouchers